I0820651

SOLUTIONS FOR A MODERN CITY
ARUP IN BEIJING

CONTENTS

前言

北京获得2008年奥运会主办权之时，很多人怀疑，北京宣称的“人文奥运、科技奥运、绿色奥运”理念是否期望值太高，但此类批评低估了北京。这个城市的中心地带为紫禁城，而紫禁城本身就是人类设计和建筑历史上最具雄心、最具标志性的项目之一。迄今为止，北京建造了一批最令人惊叹的体育场馆，但它并不满足于此，为成功举办此次盛会，还构建一整套基础设施，包括当今科技含量最高的国际机场和奥运媒体中心。

为实现奥运梦想，世界各国的优秀运动员一直在刻苦训练。为2008北京奥运搭建舞台的设计师、工程师、建筑工人也在贡献着自己的力量，帮助他们打破现有的世界纪录，确保他们拥有最好的比赛场馆，为他们营造气氛，增添力量，展现最佳状态。

这是所有人的梦想。在奥雅纳，我们感到自豪的是，在帮助将北京的梦想从概念变为现实的过程中，我们也贡献了自己的力量。如果没有我们出色的客户、合作者和同事的齐心协力，我们不可能做到这一点。

本书选择在2008年北京奥运会开幕之前出版，以纪念这个全球最伟大的运动盛会。请悉心赏读！

特瑞・希尔
主席

陈嘉正
副主席

FOREWORD

When Beijing was awarded the hosting of the 2008 Olympics, many wondered if its stated ambition to be a 'people's games, a 'high-tech' games and a 'green' games was over-ambitious. But such critics underestimated Beijing, which has at its heart the Forbidden City, itself one of the most ambitious and iconic projects ever conceived and built. Beijing was not content in creating some of the most stunning sporting structures seen to date, but also set about creating a comprehensive infrastructure to make the Games a success, including an international airport and media headquarters that are the most high-tech in the world at this time.

Great sportsmen and sportswomen in every country have been training hard to fulfil a dream. Designers, engineers, construction workers creating the stage for the 2008 Games all play a part in helping them shave that extra second from existing records, to ensure they have the best space and venue possible to give them the atmosphere and ability to achieve the best form they possibly can.

This is one dream shared by all. At Arup we are proud to have played a part in translating the vision of Beijing from a concept, to reality. We could not have done it without our wonderful clients, collaborators and colleagues.

This book is published ahead of the Beijing 2008 Olympic Games to commemorate one of the greatest sporting events in the world. Enjoy!

Terry Hill
Chairman

Andrew Chan
Deputy Chairman

SOLUTIONS FOR A MODERN CITY

STEVE ROSE

SOLUTIONS FOR A MODERN CITY

Beijing City Planning Exhibition Hall is an inconspicuous building tucked away in the southwest corner of Tiananmen Square. A low-rise, glass-fronted concrete box, it barely registers in the surrounding landscape of monumental architecture, vast open spaces and camera-toting tourists, but its contents are significant. According to the literature, the Hall is designed to "introduce the long history of the immortal city of Beijing, display the great achievements of the modern urban planning and development, and exhibit the splendid future of Beijing's urban development". Two exhibits are of particular interest, both of them microcosmic representations of the city outside. One is a ten metre-high, wall-mounted bronze relief model of Beijing circa 1949, just before Mao Zedong took control. The other is a tennis court-sized floor model showing the entire city as it will be in the near future. The city centre has been modelled in 3-D (scale 1:750). The outskirts are replicated under the floor tiles in a giant aerial photograph, so visitors can walk around and over the city and peer in awe at every detail of its transformation. You can even spot the Beijing City Planning Hall itself.

In his book *Design of Cities*, Edmund Bacon calls Beijing "possibly the greatest single work of man on the face of the earth". The city is practically a diagram of imperial China's coherent and comprehensive idea system, rendered on an unprecedented scale. Or rather a series of scales: Beijing is a fractal city—a Russian doll series of cities within cities, all obeying the same geometric principles. Looking at the bronze model, historic Beijing's underlying order is immediately apparent. From above, it is a succession of concentric quadrangles—from the outer city walls to the walls of the imperial compound at its centre. The moat and walls of the Forbidden City, the private domain of the emperor are within and are outlined in gold on the model. The basic unit of Beijing was the *siheyuan*, a four-sided single-storey residence for an extended family with an open courtyard at its centre. Neighbourhoods of *siheyuan*, known as *hutongs*, were packed neatly in a grid of streets aligned to the points of the compass. The layout of the buildings within the Forbidden City follows the same rules as the domestic architecture: courtyards within courtyards, with the most important halls and temples positioned to the north, aligned east–west, just like they are within the typical *siheyuan*. At the very heart is the emperor's throne in the Hall of Supreme Harmony, the city's most important building, where accession ceremonies, marriages and ceremonial banquets took place. All urban space is ranked in importance by its proximity to the centre.

The second ordering principle is an axis running north–south through the centre of the city. This line of power starts at the Gate of Eternal Stability, the south entrance to Beijing, either side of which, immediately within the city walls, were a temple of agriculture and the round Temple of Heaven, which still stands. The axis passes through Tiananmen Square, through the centre of the Forbidden City (and therefore its most important structures), and up beyond it to the ceremonial bell and drum towers, in the north of the city.

The difference between these two models is striking, especially when one considers it took just 60 years to get from one to the other. The 1949 one could just as easily be from the fifteenth century. The Beijing it records differed little from that of the Ming and Qing emperors who ruled it for the previous 500 years. Beyond the city walls, there is practically nothing. The second model, by contrast, displays as contemporary a cityscape as it is possible to imagine: skyscrapers; ten-lane highways; the new forms of the Olympic venues; and transparent blocks on sites where buildings have yet to be constructed. But despite the transformation, the underlying pattern is still visible. The Forbidden City is still there at the centre, of course. And although the city walls were almost entirely demolished in the 1960s, their course can still be traced in the route of

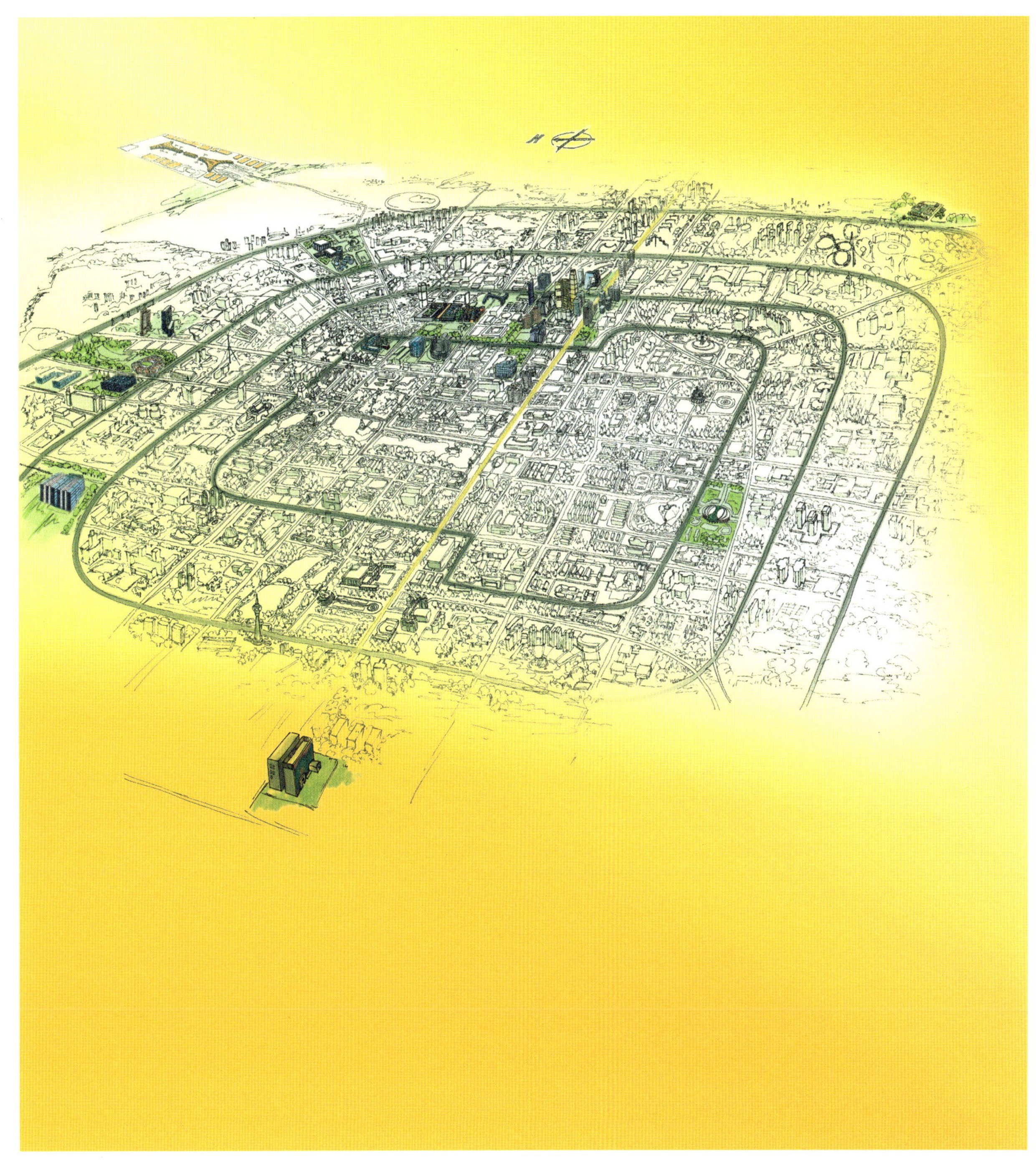

The layout of modern Beijing, highlighting some of Arup's major projects in the city.

the Second Ring Road, which replaced them. A further series of ring roads, up to the sixth now, have extended the city perimeter far beyond its imperial limits; but they have reinforced Beijing's pattern of concentric quadrangles. Similarly, the central north–south axis has now been extended to the north, along the central promenade of the new Olympic Green.

Beyond the transformation, there is something remarkable about the very existence of the Beijing City Planning Hall. It is difficult to imagine any other city (except perhaps Shanghai) making such great efforts to visualise and represent its past and future so thoroughly. The 1949-era model was cast from 9.7 tons of bronze. The floor model is painstakingly detailed, even down to the wooden mullions between the window panes, and took more than 150 workers almost a year to construct. In addition the museum contains interactive displays and even an in-house cinema offering a 3-D virtual reality flythrough of the new city. In most cities, development is neither sufficiently interesting nor co-ordinated to justify such a conscientious public display, but Beijing possesses both the will and the means to present its own emergence with utter certitude. Here is a city narrating its story to itself.

Beijing is certainly ready for its close-up. There is a sense the city has been steadily positioning itself for a central role in twenty-first century geopolitics for some time. It is surely Beijing's turn. In the 1980s, Hong Kong was the city to marvel at—the gateway to the 'new China'. In the 1990s, the focus shifted to Shanghai, where a new forest of skyscrapers marked the city's economic resurgence. But now Beijing has the momentum. Not only is its own commercial base growing, its position as the cultural, historical, educational and political centre of China is undeniable. As is China's ascendance as a global superpower: the world's most populous country, the world's largest manufacturing nation, the world's largest army, the fastest-growing major economy for the past 25 years, the superlatives go on. It is estimated that half of all the construction work currently taking place in the world is happening in China. Its growth is unprecedented and, apparently, unstoppable. "With a mixture of concern and fascination, all eyes are focused on China", writes Rem Koolhaas, an architect who has studied contemporary China in considerable depth. "[It is] perhaps the greatest gamble in the history of mankind, it is a gamble that no one can afford [China] to lose."

The XXIX Olympiad, then, is the moment when Beijing lays its cards on the table. The city will be visited by a predicted 4.5 million foreign tourists in 2008, and the Olympic Games will be viewed on television by an estimated four billion people around the world. In addition, some 30,000 journalists are coming to town to report on the Olympics themselves. When all eyes are firmly focused on China, what will they see?

When the city's officials first asked themselves this question, they cannot have been very satisfied with the answer. That would have been in the early 1990s, in the run-up to Beijing's bid to host the 2000 Olympics, which it narrowly lost to Sydney. At that time, China was not well placed to win any global popularity contests. Nor was the city itself in great shape. What visitors would have seen had there been a Beijing Olympics in 2000 would probably not have impressed them. By the late 1990s Beijing had already set off down the same path as every other Chinese city, embracing a standard model of no-questions-asked modernism with the primary objective of keeping pace with its mushrooming urban population. With speed and profit, the priorities—design quality considerations and conservation issues—were relegated. Across China, the early economic boom was marked by the erection of soulless high-rise apartment complexes and flashy mirror-glassed commercial towers. "Many cities have a similar construction style", complained Vice Construction Minister Qiu Baoxing in 2007. "It is like a thousand cities having the same appearance."

Beijing was never in danger of falling into total anonymity, but while the most conspicuous historic sites such as the Forbidden City and Temple of Heaven (both of which are UNESCO World Heritage Sites) acted as islands of stability, the ancient urban fabric surrounding them, the *hutongs*, were rapidly being replaced by higher density housing to accommodate the steady flow of migrant workers pouring in to the capital. The familiar matte of architectural blandness had started to spread over the city itself. Furthermore, Beijing was blighted by heavy air pollution from factories and coal-fired power stations within the city itself, and the inexorable growth of motor traffic was pushing its transport infrastructure towards permanent gridlock.

When Beijing was awarded the 2008 Olympics in 2001, the question of what foreign eyes would see was still hanging. "They will not only report on the Games. They will scrutinise every tiny feature of the city and report back to their home countries", said Wang Qishan, mayor of Beijing in 2005. "If they find smelly back street toilets, stinking rivers and litter everywhere, what would the people make of Beijing and China?"

"New Beijing, Great Olympics" was the city's official slogan when it was competing to host the games, but where was the new Beijing? Innumerable initiatives were launched to address and improve air pollution,

An artist's impression of the China World Trade Center Phase 3 standing tall in the central business district.

sanitation, public transport, even civic politeness, but how could the world perceive a 'New Beijing' when the city's most noteworthy structures had been built hundreds of years previously? What would the TV cameras cut to between the sporting events? To put it bluntly, the New Beijing needed symbols. It needed design-led signifiers of its twenty-first century status. The very idea of symbolic design is somewhat outmoded in a jaded post-industrial society, but Beijing's course of action attests to its power as both medium and message.

The word 'iconic' in connection with design tends to arouse suspicion these days. Sooner or later when dealing with these types of one-off showpieces, someone is sure to invoke the 'Guggenheim effect', referring to Frank Gehry's now world-famous Guggenheim Museum Bilbao, a flamboyant structure of swirling titanium that has become Exhibit A in any definition of 'iconic' architecture. Few people were familiar with the northeastern Spanish city of Bilbao before the Guggenheim opened in 1997; now it is firmly on the cultural map, visited by significantly higher numbers of tourists, the majority of whom come with the express intention of seeing Gehry's building. Mid-ranking cities across the world have attempted to emulate the Guggenheim effect, commissioning renowned foreign 'starchitects' to design them prestigious urban centrepieces—usually museums and art galleries—in the hope of catapulting themselves into public consciousness. Far more often than not, such bare-faced icon-building has backfired, failing to benefit the host city as anticipated and raising scepticism of architects as glorified public relations consultants.

Should we categorise Beijing's Olympic structures in this context? It could be argued that the city is, in fact, doing the opposite of Bilbao and its imitators. Rather than seeking to elevate its position through iconic designs, Beijing was seeking iconic designs to match its existing position. By any measure Beijing was already a city 'on the map'; it just needed the type of architecture one would expect of a world city. A 'reverse Guggenheim', if you will.

None of the projects covered in this book could be mistaken for mere exercises in symbolism. After all, Beijing needed to build. With the Olympics as an imminent reality, there were well-defined objectives to fulfil from a design perspective—and a fixed schedule for achieving them. Beijing needed the full complement of world-class sports venues and support facilities to host the Games. It needed the infrastructure to cope with the influx of visitors—an efficient, integrated public transport system, hotels, restaurants, conference facilities and so forth. But these large, new pieces of design in the cityscape had no option but to represent the city, and by extension the country. So what is Beijing communicating with its recent commissions? What could we reasonably interpret from this set of projects?

To start with, the sheer scale of these projects is an unambiguous indicator of Beijing's ambition. Timidity was clearly not on the agenda. By and large, these are enormous structures, large enough to alter the material landscape of one of the world's largest cities. The 74-storey China World Trade Center Phase 3, for example, is the tallest building in a city whose seismic conditions inhibit the erection of high structures. Beijing South Rail Station will be the largest train station in Asia. The headquarters of China Central Television (CCTV) is one of the largest office buildings on earth. Years before they were constructed, they were already communicating the scale of Beijing's ambition in the form of statistics and superlatives. What observer could fail to be amazed, for example, by news that 50,000 people were working to construct Beijing Capital International Airport's new Terminal 3, that it would be the world's largest and most advanced airport building, or that it could comfortably house all five terminals of London's Heathrow Airport?

View of the National Stadium and its reflection, showing its 'Bird's Nest'-like structure.

By extension, design on this scale demands and therefore denotes considerable financial resources. Few can ignore the fact that the scope of Beijing's Olympic undertaking signifies an economy in robust health. Cheaper, less difficult alternatives could have been selected. One need only compare Herzog & de Meuron's pioneering design for Beijing's National Stadium, also known as the 'Bird's Nest', with the modest, almost temporary stadium proposed for the London Olympics in 2012. To be fair, construction costs in Beijing are approximately a tenth of those in London, thanks to cheaper labour and materials, so expenditure is not a reliable indicator. Still, China has not shied away from flaunting some degree of affluence. Beijing's own official estimate for the Olympics' budget is US$ two billion, although outside estimates of China's total indirect spend in preparation for the Games have been as high as US$ 50 billion.

However, it would be simplistic to reduce Beijing's mission to a straightforward show of strength. Building big is a straightforward option for nations striving to make their mark, but size for its own sake sends out a rather hollow message. It is interesting to compare Beijing to Dubai, for example, which currently trumps all newcomers in terms of new-build statistics, starting with Burj Dubai, currently the world's tallest building. There is a sense in Dubai that the numbers are setting the agenda, that by chasing the unrivalled, the city is attempting to build itself into significance (one could have said the same for Kuala Lumpur and its Petronas Towers, previous holder of the 'world's tallest building' title). Beijing, by contrast, has taken a different approach. The city's new works meet or surpass current design standards, and in some cases they transcend them altogether. It is no exaggeration to state that Beijing is home to some of the most exciting and radical design statements of the twenty-first century. The eyes of the world have been trained on Beijing for some time, drawn by the number of prominent designers working in the city, and the otherworldly structures emerging there.

It is true that many of these structures make an immediate visual impact. Many of them could be characterised by the overt expression of their 'newness', starting with the National Stadium, a building where facade and structure have fused into a seamless whole. But these buildings are not exercises in mere 'shapism'.

Take the National Aquatics Center, or the 'Water Cube', the venue for the Olympic swimming events.

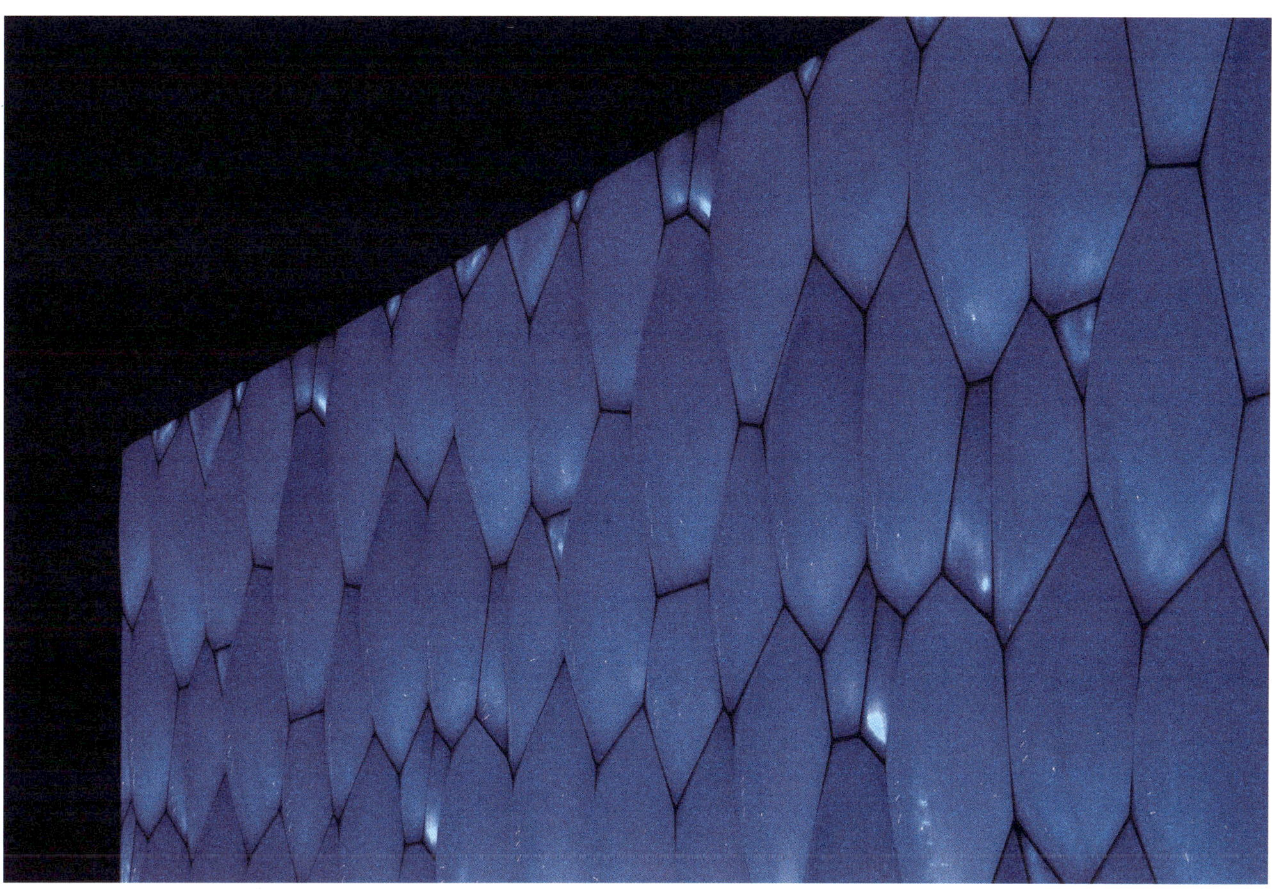

"It can be read on many levels", says Arup's principal designer on the project, Tristram Carfrae.

> There's the simple thing that it is full of water and looks like a box of bubbles. But actually the next step down, the geometry of it is the theoretical geometry of an infinite array of a set of bubbles. So it is not just a pastiche; there is a purity to it. Underneath that, again, is a reason for that: a purpose—that is, to produce a structure that is fantastically, seismically resistant and that can heat the pools and produce an acoustic [effect].

In a similar way, the new headquarters for CCTV presents itself as a new type of structure in the cityscape, but not an arbitrary one. Rather, it is the result of nearly 20 years of investigation on the part of architects OMA and engineers Arup into the possibilities of the 'hyper-building', a self-sustaining city-within-a-city that offers an alternative to the vertical impasse of the skyscraper for very large buildings. Previous incarnations of the 'hyper-building' had been proposed for Seoul and Bangkok, explains Arup's Rory McGowan, but only Beijing has been bold enough to explore this untested building type (a city-within-a-city—how apt for Beijing, a fractal city). Far more than just a symbol of the new city, it is a revolutionary structure in the history of architecture. "I don't really see it as Chinese", says McGowan.

> I don't see it as a Beijing project... I think it is truly international. The whole project is all about questioning the future of density in cities—it is questioning the slavery of admiration towards skyscrapers where there's only one method of circulation and that is up and down. And it is going to be a debating point for decades, there is no doubt about that.

This disposition towards mold-breaking, agenda-setting architecture challenges long-established preconceptions about China's relationship with modernity, conformity and creative thinking. "The Chinese aren't shocked by avant-garde designs", stated Jacques Herzog of Herzog & de Meuron. "Actually, they are very pragmatic and thoughtful about them." The decision to employ international design firms transmits a message of openness and co-operation that is contrary to the closed-door mentality of 'old China' and in keeping with Beijing's overall Olympic aspirations.

(Opposite) Construction shot showing the roof and bowl design of the National Stadium.

(Above) A night view of the National Aquatics Center, also known as the 'Water Cube'.

决策
MEETING
行政区
NEWS
新媒体
PRODUCTION
FOOD COURT
制作
CCTV
新闻区
演播室
STUDIO
入口大堂

An early artist's impression of China Central Television headquarters from the competition submission. CCTV is China's principal state-run broadcaster and currently has 13 channels. It plans to operate over 200 channels in the near future, competing with CNN, NBC, Sky, and the BBC in the global market. To enable this expansion, and to place CCTV firmly on the global map, an iconic new headquarters facility was needed, with the entire television-making process housed in one location within Beijing's newly-designated central business district.

The message of Beijing's makeover is not purely intended for the international community, it bears emphasising; it is also being received by the Chinese people themselves. Beijing is in competition with other Chinese cities, particularly Shanghai. "It is a very strong message to people living and working in Beijing that it is not such a conservative city any more", says Michael Kwok, a Director at Arup.

> That is important because if you ask some of the younger people in China, "which city do you want to work in?" a lot of them will say Shanghai because it is seen as a place where people can develop and grow freely. Beijing has been associated with officials and controls and seen as very regulatory, but the buildings we are witnessing are changing that view. I think we will see an acceleration of creativity coming out of the city. A lot of research and development centres are being set up in Beijing by various organisations, a lot of intellectual property creatives are pushing boundaries and experimenting there. It is quite important for China to have a city that is able to accept new concepts, new ideas and go beyond conventions, so I think the iconic architecture we are seeing will be very good for Beijing in the long term.

Having readied itself for the Olympics, is Beijing ready for the hangover? What happens after the closing ceremony? We have discussed how this set of projects transform the meaning and image of Beijing; their legacy is yet more vital. Do they have a role to play in an emergent Chinese urban identity?

Beijing's architectural mission might appear to be ambitious but it is not unprecedented. In modern times the Olympic movement has often been characterised by heroic design. As the torch has passed from city to city, so has a legacy of construction experimentation and innovation. As with the 'Bird's Nest' and the 'Water Cube', Olympic venues have historically attempted to be at the frontier of structural possibility. The modern era was initiated with the XVII Olympiad of 1960, in Rome, for example, where architect/engineer Pier Luigi Nervi supplied a trio of pioneering venues, including the *Stadio Olympico*, a genuine monument to modernism, with a roof canopy supported by elegant, slender cantilevered beams of reinforced concrete. The 1972 Olympics, in Munich, brought to global attention the futuristic tensile structures of Frei Otto, who erected a 135-metre cable-net roof over Günther Behnisch's stadium. In the pre-computer era, Otto's forms were arrived at through a complex process involving models, soap bubbles and mathematical formulae, but the result was a striking lightweight canopy. More recently, Spanish genius, Santiago Calatrava, provided a dramatic set of structures for the Athens Olympics in 2000, including the spectacular revamp of an existing stadium and a lightweight open promenade reminiscent of giant leaves. His dynamic white-steel structures were so ambitious, they were dismissed as impossible by many before they were built.

Two recent Olympic events, in particular, make for interesting comparisons with Beijing 2008: Tokyo 1964 and Barcelona 1992. In the case of the Tokyo games, Japan's position in 1964 was roughly comparable to Beijing's today: entering into the international community in earnest after a period of alienation; in the throes of an economic boom; experiencing unprecedented urban growth and unpredictable social transformation. The architectural stars of the event were a matching pair of structures, a gymnasium and a swimming centre, designed by Kenzo Tange. Beautifully gestural but rigorously functional, capped by elegant shell-like catenary steel roofs, Tange's buildings seemed to encapsulate the country's aspirations. Tange came to be regarded as one of the twentieth century's greatest form-givers, and out of his office came a new generation of Japanese design talent, including Arata Isozaki, Fumihiko Maki and Kisho Kurokawa.

Barcelona, like Beijing, seized the opportunity of the Olympics to update the city's neglected infrastructure at an accelerated rate. Under the direction of Oriol Bohigus, the Spanish city integrated its Olympic construction programme into a comprehensive urban development plan that called for the creation of public parks and plazas. A new generation of architectural landmarks was also added to the city—such as Calatrava's unmistakeable Telecommunications Tower, or Rafael Moneo's new airport.

Comparing Beijing to these two events raises further questions. Should China, like Japan, have used the Olympics to promote its own design talent? Should Beijing, like Barcelona, have used its Olympics to rectify more of the city's shortcomings?

Neither question is new. The hangover had already started before the Games themselves began. By 2004, debates were already going on as to whether or not it was appropriate to be spending such large amounts on the Olympics, and employing so many international designers. Accusations were levelled that China had simply been on a shopping spree for prestige architectural brand-names—Norman Foster, Rem Koolhaas, Herzog & de Meuron, Terry Farrell, and so forth—without really considering what it was getting. In response, a number of internationally-designed projects in the city were called in by the government for cost review in 2004. Changes were demanded in some—the removal of the sliding roof from the 'Bird's Nest', for example. Others, such as a planned commercial neighbourhood designed by Zaha Hadid, were cancelled.

The presence of foreign designers and engineers in China has inevitably generated resentment among some local architects, particularly those of the older generation. "Some cities in China have become 'experimental sites' for both noted foreign architects and some second- and third-level ones", complained Wu Liangyong, Professor of Architecture at Beijing's Tsinghua University, in 2004. "These buildings will be a scar left on the face of time, which will record our pains for ever."

Companies like Arup do not see it that way, Michael Kwok explains. Kwok established Arup's Beijing office in 2001, but the company had been active in mainland China since 1984, and had participated in some 500 construction projects across the country. But working in China is always a genuine collaboration, Kwok points out. Foreign architectural and engineering firms in China must work jointly with a domestic counterpart: a local 'design institute'. So with every project, expertise is steadily being transferred from the foreign companies to the domestic professionals (and vice versa). "The local desire to work with foreign designers is quite profound", Kwok says. "For most of the projects we have worked on in China we have found our relationship with the locals to be very good. We found in most cases we can agree on common goals and have a synergy working together."

From the other side, Beijing architect Zhu Pei agrees. Zhu designed Digital Beijing, the media command centre for the Olympics, a striking, black-clad building resembling a giant electronic component, situated close to the 'Water Cube'. "If you review the architecture and infrastructure built in China before the 1990s, it was mostly done without any urban consideration", Zhu says.

> So, probably after about 2000, a lot of people realised we needed to bring new concepts into Chinese urban development. Projects like the 'Bird's Nest' or CCTV have had a really positive impact on the landscape, but they have also stimulated the local design institutes' approach. Maybe some people have criticised these foreigners 'experimenting' in Beijing but to me, they are not only bringing new architecture, they are bringing totally new approaches, new concepts about what architecture should be. How buildings can respect people and respect the environment and provide meaning. I think that is a positive thing.

For an international city like Beijing, solutions from home and abroad are needed. Besides which, the distinction between the two is becoming less relevant. Contemporary Chinese design is still in its infancy, says Zhu, but it is developing apace. Only since 1983 have architects like him been allowed to set up studios on their own, independent of the local design institutes. Now there are a number of names making their mark, in China and beyond. Zhu is currently designing a new Guggenheim Art Pavilion in Abu Dhabi, which will sit alongside buildings by Zaha Hadid, Jean Nouvel and Frank Gehry. Like Zhu, most of the new generation of Chinese architects have been schooled in Europe and North America, as well as at home. Beijing-born Chang Yung Ho, for example, studied and practised in the US before returning to set up Atelier FCJZ, the city's first private architectural firm. He currently divides his time between local projects and the Massachusetts Institute of Technology, where he heads the architecture department. Similarly, Qing Yun Ma graduated from Beijing's Tsinghua University then completed his studies in the US. He is now Dean of the University of Southern California's school of architecture, while his Shanghai-based company MADA spam is involved in planning and architecture projects across China. The list goes on.

Post-Olympics, the challenge these designers face is to forge the chaotic, contradictory forces of China's development into a viable form of urbanism. In a city like Beijing, that challenge is exacerbated by its unique historic and contemporary conditions. As we have seen, Beijing was never designed as a city in the Western sense. In most European cities the ruling monarchy or aristocracy was one of several centres of power, others including the church and the merchant classes. Tensions between them shaped the urban landscape. In Beijing, there was no power other than that of the emperor. All forms of activity in the city, from politics to trade to art and culture, were conducted in his name and subservient to his authority. The city was effectively a giant palace. Even when Mao Zedong and his forces took control of Beijing in 1949, they never set out to create a genuine city. Instead, Mao divided Beijing into discrete 'work-units', between which citizens had little freedom of movement. In all likelihood, Beijingers would live, work, eat, go to school and probably even marry within their work-unit, and would rarely leave it. Rather than a city, Beijing was more like a collection of adjacent neighbourhoods.

Modern-day Beijing is still a divided city. Not only are districts now socially and economically separate from each other due to the city's capitalist dynamics; they are physically separated by ten-lane highways. One fundamental change is underway already: Beijing's metro system has been expanding across the city, and will continue to do so well beyond the Olympics. By 2020 it is expected to be the largest in the world.

Sensitive additions above the ground—what Zhu Pei calls "urban acupuncture"—can make a difference. One existing example could be Jianwai SOHO, a high-end commercial and residential complex two miles east of Tiananmen Square. Conceived by Beijing-born Japanese architect Riken Yamamoto, it is a collection of white, uniform, high-rise towers that could almost have been designed by arch-modernist Mies van der Rohe. But Jianwai SOHO is unique among Beijing developments in that it strives to create a genuine pedestrian urban realm. Traffic is kept out of the centre of the site, so it is possible to walk between buildings. Another proposal, by American architect Steven Holl, entitled Looped Hybrid Housing, follows the lead set by OMA's CCTV 'hyper-building'. If realised, it would create a science-fiction landscape of eight residential high-rises connected both at the ground and by soaring bridges at the 20th floor level—'streets in the sky'. A city within the city.

For many designers and planners, the clearest way forward is the city's past, found in the traditional *hutongs*, the low-rise neighbourhoods of courtyard houses that historically formed the residential focus of the city. As the bronze model in the Beijing City Planning Exhibition illustrates, even in 1949, almost the entire city outside the central imperial compound was made up of these *hutongs*. Within these narrow, pedestrian alleyways neighbourhood interaction and genuine street life has prevailed throughout China's turbulent history. But in the past few decades the *hutongs* have been disappearing at an unprecedented rate. According to UNESCO, one third of central Beijing's old city has been razed in the last three years, displacing more than 500,000 people. It would be easy to romanticise the past and ignore the fact that most homes in the *hutongs* had no modern plumbing and relied on public toilets, or that most of the historic courtyard houses had been subdivided and added to over the years to the extent that they were all but unsalvageable. But still, the current generation of Chinese designers is returning to the *hutong* model, either directly preserving and restoring existing historic neighbourhoods, or building anew, using the urban vitality of the *hutongs* as the basis for new, culturally-Chinese housing typologies.

As we have seen, Beijing has changed from imperial relic to front-running global city in a single generation. China's capital is putting on a confident smile for its Olympic 'coming-out' party but, deep down, one could forgive the city for feeling a little bewildered by its present condition. The past and the future are not yet too far apart to reconnect, though. The city's underlying order has proved impossible to eradicate, and its weaknesses will not be impossible to rectify. One senses that a pause would be helpful, that Beijing needs time to catch up with its own narrative before it can contemplate the next chapter. For the foreseeable future, however, China's momentum will permit no time for reflection. No great city can be in full control of its own destiny. There are still many ways the map of the future Beijing can be drawn, and as long as that remains the case, we'll still all be watching—and contributing.

THE ART OF AESTHETIC ENGINEERING

DAN HEWITT

THE ART OF AESTHETIC ENGINEERING

Walter Gropius, grandfather of 'modern' architecture, once wrote: "Ideas perish as soon as they are compromised.... To build in fantasy without regard for technical difficulties; to have the gift of imagination is more important than all technology, which adapts itself to man's creative will".[1]

Looking at most of Arup's projects in Beijing—whether as lead designers or engineers—Gropius would surely be content. In terms of sheer creativity and audaciousness, they appear to have been "built in fantasy". Without the "gift of imagination" they would not exist. Yet to set "man's creative will" entirely in opposition to "technology" is to do both a disservice. Such exceptionally imaginative structures are made into reality not by "technology adapting itself to man's creative will" but through productive collaboration between architects, engineers and designers.

The ethos of Arup as an organisation is principally about collaborative endeavour. The idea that the creativity is in the idea—and that technology is subordinate, faceless and essentially mechanical—is a misrepresentation of the future of building design and contrary to the ethos of Arup. The firm's visionary founder, Sir Ove Arup, coined the expression "Total Architecture" to describe the need for each profession involved in the design and construction of a building to come together at the project's inception, collectively to define the way forward.

Arup's perspective departed from the traditional view of the design process as a sequence of discrete responsibilities undertaken independently of, and in reaction to, decisions made by others earlier on in the process.[2] As a result, while the professional competencies of architects, structural engineers, services engineers, quantity surveyors and services contractors may remain distinct, considerable scope exists for each party to influence the overall design. This is particularly evident in a number of Arup's Beijing projects, in which the firm's engineers, designers and consultants have played significant roles in developing and defining the aesthetic character of those buildings.

Furthermore, the idea of some kind of hierarchy of importance between aesthetic creativity and technology is somewhat pretentious. It is plain that both are necessary conditions for successful architecture. Technology enables just as much as it limits the imagination, as can be seen in Beijing's National Aquatics Center, also known as the 'Water Cube', where technology provided the means to realise what otherwise would have remained a mere 'idea'. Arup's Beijing projects repeatedly blur any preconceived boundaries between artistic and technical imagination. "The rise of the engineer", as it has been dubbed, has been consistent throughout the latter half of the twentieth century. A brief outline of certain aspects of this phenomenon may therefore help give context to a more detailed account of the way Arup has worked in Beijing.[3]

The emphasis on unhindered creativity in Gropius' statement described at the beginning of this text is alluring, yet curiously empty: a brilliant idea is, as he acknowledged, essentially ephemeral. Ove

(Left) Aerial view of construction of CCTV after the building was topped out.

(Right) The 'Bird's Nest' glows softly in the reflected dusk light.

Arup himself was famous for providing the technical solutions to the daring forms envisaged by many of his architect collaborators. His partnership with architect Berthold Lubetkin is notable in this respect. This may at first appear to support Gropius' fantasy, of "technology adapting itself to man's creative will". However, as critic Andrew Saint observes, Arup's deference of technique to art could work only if the architect showed an intelligent respect towards technology.[4] For example, an architect who intends to sculpt in novel ways a material such as concrete—which can be cast into a wide variety of forms such as columns, beams, slabs, panels, shells—needs to take expert advice from a structural engineer right at the outset. It would be no good completing the design and then simply handing it to the engineer, instructing him or her to make it stand up. This kind of problem beset the Sydney Opera House project. The architect, Jørn Utzon, won the 1957 competition to design the Opera House without either the jury or himself consulting any engineers about its structural feasibility—the kind of oversight guarded against by design competitions worldwide ever since. After Ove Arup was appointed to the project, he and his team worked patiently with the young architect trying to find ways to make his designs feasible and, when they could not, suggesting alternative methods fully supported by Utzon. However, Utzon handed his resignation in before the Opera House was completed.

The story behind the Sydney Opera House highlights a significant shift that has taken place: the displacement—not replacement—of the architect by the engineer. Architects will always be needed for their artistic skills, but almost every aspect of the design implementation is a matter for engineers.[5]

The traditional relationship between engineer and architect is thus characterised as one requiring mutual respect, but one which nevertheless places the engineer in a primarily subservient role to the architect's vision. However, as so-called "High-Tech" architects in the second half of the twentieth century became interested in the aesthetics of engineering structures, the visibility of the engineers' 'technique' elevated it into an art.[6] Felix Samuely's Frank Newby articulated this apparent overlap between the roles of engineer and architect as follows:

> In architecture, the structure is only part of the whole; it is the architect who is creating the image and the environment. He may not welcome or accept ideas from the engineer. However, the fine tuning and sculpting of exposed structural elements and joints are often left to the engineer and the quality of such details comes from his experience and flair.[7]

On occasion, the impetus for the project could even start with the engineers. For example, the winning competition entry to design the Centre Pompidou in Paris originated with engineers at Arup who were experts in space frames and lightweight structures. Because the competition rules required them to work under an architect, they cajoled Richard Rogers and Renzo Piano to join their team. Although the final design owed much to the hard work of Rogers and Piano after the terms of the contract with the French government changed mid-way through the project, it was Arup's engineers who, among many other novel achievements, initiated the use of the exposed steel scaffolding and fashioned the 'gerberettes'. The latter are "plump, pivoting, cantilevered castings exposed outside the building envelope, which connect the 48 metre span main beams of the floors to the main columns and, beyond them at the outermost edge, with vertical tension rods. They do a critical job and are therefore engineer's details."[8]

However, some engineers express ambivalence about the role they played in High-Tech architecture. Widely regarded as the first High-Tech building to be built, the Reliance Controls factory in Swindon, 1965–1966, was largely designed by its engineer Tony Hunt, in partnership with the architects Team 4 (Norman

and Wendy Foster and Richard and Su Rogers). The points of unease came in Foster's suggestion to display structural elements which were superfluous and to leave them out where they were obviously necessary. Hunt recounts:

> The point that I always have to answer for now is the multiple cross-bracing, not only along the sides that would have required some diagonal support anyway, but also along the two elevations… that did not require it at all. I am still a little embarrassed: it is not a 'pure' structure, so the engineer in me can never be entirely satisfied. The designer in me, however, tends to agree that it makes the building look better. The real irony—and for me a far more difficult problem—was that Norman, who had used all his charm to persuade me to accept the multiple cross-bracing for the building, then decided the water tower would be better without it. As a very tall, very slender portal frame, this really did present some problems![9]

The ensuing widespread use of pseudo-structural gestures by High-Tech architects was at odds with many engineers' conception of themselves as the providers of the most efficient technical solution to a structural problem. As a result, the High-Tech style became somewhat maligned among the engineering profession, not only because engineers were required to produce inefficient structures, but because in doing so they had to spend a great deal of time designing redundant structural details that did not present any kind of intellectual challenge as Frank Newby was to complain:

> Architects just started using structure as decoration and, because it carried load, we had to deal with it. It made a lot of extra work. But if you are asking me whether High-Tech architecture advanced technology in any way, I would have to say no. It made no contribution at all. There was nothing in all of it half as testing as the problems of a long span bridge or a decent sized stadium.[10]

Similar sentiments were taken to an extreme in 2006 by German engineer Jorg Schlaich, who would denounce any structure which does not solve a functional problem—such as providing a stadium for 100,000 spectators "as economically as possible, using the least possible materials. [Structure] should never be subjugated to art… whatever art is".[11] His view is that the 'art' of architecture should not create problems that require structural engineering solutions. This is distinct from nineteenth century critic John Ruskin's demand that architecture should not contain elements that deceive by pretending to be structural.[12] Ruskin's concern was with genuine structure as a symbol of honesty. The objecting engineer's concerns

(Opposite) At night the illuminated 'Water Cube' reveals a magnificent view of its bubble-like facade.

(Above) Construction photograph showing details of the grid design feature which gave the Stadium its nickname the 'Bird's Nest'.

appear to be with efficiency—a matter of professional principle which, in some cases, seems to be elevated to one of morality—and avoiding the personal boredom of producing ornaments when they could be putting their skills to more demanding work.

Whilst Schlaich's position may appear a little obsessive, many engineers place great importance on efficiency. However, unrelenting structural efficiency appears to threaten aesthetic ambition. Partly in response to these concerns, Arup's Cecil Balmond developed a strikingly different approach. First of all, he takes issue with "formal" engineering solutions and with structures that are "comprehensible and explicit", describing formality as structure that "marches to strict rhythms". "Is space so dull", he asks, "that punctuating it means only the regular monotonous beat of verticals and horizontals?"[13] He retains the engineer's concern for efficiency, but believes that the most efficient solution is circumscribed by artistic aims. Sometimes, he says, an offbeat structure may yield a more efficient solution than the "unquestioned assumption of a distributed solution, subdivided equally through cross section or plan". This brings him into line with Ove Arup's original ethos of seeking to provide the most efficient structural solution to an artistic vision. However, it is often difficult to see who is taking the artistic lead in Balmond's collaborations with architects such as Rem Koolhaas on Rotterdam's Kunsthal, Peter Kulka and Ulrich Königs on Chemnitz Sports Stadium, and Daniel Libeskind on the 'Spiral' structure and 'Fractile' pattern for the Victoria and Albert Museum, London. What is notable is that Balmond talks of his desire for space to entertain us:

> Why not relax and move towards a skip and a jump in the arrangement of things? Let the informal in. Have a syncopation—a rat-ta-ta-tat—instead of the dull metronomic one-two repeat of post and beam that rises up and runs along our buildings in stark structural skeletons.[14]

He points out that there is no decree that obliges us to think of structure as "the basic functional skeleton or the manifest of a high-tech machine".[15] Instead, he is interested in the visibility of structure and its capacity to be dynamic, subtle, ambiguous—or even unsettling—in its appearance.

The development of each Beijing project had its own dynamic, but artistry and technical expertise are especially intertwined in the National Aquatics Center, China Central Television's headquarters (CCTV), the National Stadium (known as the 'Bird's Nest'), and, in subtler ways, Beijing Capital International Airport Terminal 3. On the one hand, each employs structural elements as architectural devices but, unlike the projects lamented by Newby, these have tested

the engineers' imaginations, analytical abilities and, in important respects, their aesthetic creativity. On the other hand, the question of efficiency remains vexed. For example, the 'Bird's Nest' uses 20 times more steel per square metre than the Airport, and while CCTV's steel rate (250 kilograms per square metre of floor space) does not compare unfavourably with other similar-sized tall buildings in seismic regions—and indeed makes important savings—the unusual form of the building has required a large volume of steel to stabilise it.[16] It is not that the engineering of the chosen designs could be more efficient; rather, if the form of the building were different, then the structure could be engineered in an alternative way and thereby use less material. Granting primacy to an architectural vision can therefore sometimes compromise other ideals. Nevertheless, what is interesting in Arup's projects is how engineers have been instrumental in developing the 'art' in these architectural wonders. Since each project had a unique form of collaboration and different set of requirements in the brief, it is necessary to recount them individually.

The 'Water Cube' represents an exemplary fusion of architectural and engineering innovation. The

aesthetic effect is mesmerising, yet the structure is efficient. Both effects sprang from a set of highly-constrained functional requirements, identified by Arup and the Australian architects PTW. The firms are long-time collaborators on international swimming centres, such as the Sydney Olympic pool. First, the building needed to be able to maintain a high, even temperature throughout the year. When swimmers exit swimming pools, water on their skin quickly evaporates consuming body heat, thus making them more vulnerable to cold air temperatures. The annual temperature range in Beijing is wide: the average minimum temperature in January is 10 degrees Centigrade (C) and average maximum temperature in June is 30 degrees C. However, the temperature can drop to minus 23 degrees C in winter and soar to 43 degrees C in summer.[17] Secondly, the internal surface needed to be as acoustically permeable as possible, as the hard tiled surfaces of swimming centres reflect, rather than absorb sound. Given the scale of the 'Water Cube' and the number of cheering spectators that it can accommodate, noise levels would have been horrendous if the walls and the ceiling were also hard. Thirdly, the structure needed to be outside the pool hall, because when chlorine gas mixes with water vapour, it produces hydrochloric acid, which would quickly corrode any exposed steel.

(Opposite top) View of the railway station at Beijing Capital International Airport Terminal 3, which connects the airport with the city centre.

(Opposite bottom left) View of the Chinese Central Television's (CCTV) headquarters site from the northeast, taken on the day in December 2007 when the towers were connected to form a continuous loop.

(Opposite bottom right) Workers on the roof of the 'Bird's Nest'.

(Above) The 'Water Cube' at night.

An insulated greenhouse capable of reducing solar glare was conceived as the natural solution. Inevitably, the greenhouse material chosen was not glass but ethylene tetra fluoro ethylene (ETFE) a clear plastic, which is a kind of Teflon developed in Germany in the early 1980s. ETFE has a number of advantages: it allows more visible light to pass through it than glass; it is arranged in air-filled pillows that act as an insulating layer; the fritted surface prevents glare; it is acoustically transparent, meaning that sound largely passes straight through it rather than being reflected; and because of its non-stick properties, it cleans itself whenever it rains.

With a view to maximising the space available for post-Games use, it was decided that the building would occupy all of its square site. The architects had noticed the prevalence of square and circular forms, together with red and blue colours, in traditional Chinese architecture. At around the same time, the winning design for the National Stadium was announced. Since that building was rounded and red (signifying heaven in traditional Chinese culture) it seemed natural to make the contrasting Aquatic Centre box-shaped in elevation and plan, and blue in colour, signifying earth.[18]

(Opposite) A detail of the ETFE cladding system used in the 'Water Cube'.

(Above) The steel and glass facade of the China World Trade Center Phase 3.

(Right) Installation of a post-fixed brace for the CCTV building.

The general kind of form and specific materials required for the project could therefore be specified in some detail before the team even began producing design proposals. The aesthetic challenge, of course, was how to present this box in an interesting way. The standard structural solution of a triangulated space frame was immediately ruled out, since it would not have been sufficiently striking for the pre-eminent international competition. With a ten-week timescale, four passed without any satisfactory design being put forward. The team initially worked on the idea of a roof structure composed of vertical steel tubes clad with circular ETFE panels, but this presented two problems: firstly, circles do not fit together exactly, but leave awkward voids; and secondly, the vertical tubes in the ceiling would not intersect with horizontal tubes in the walls in an elegant way. This prompted Arup engineer, Tristram Carfrae, to wonder what kinds of structures go around corners or 'inhabit' space uniformly, besides the uninspiring triangulated space-frame?

Nature might have provided the answer but, despite the number of cellular or mineral examples that exist, there was no straightforward way of translating these into geometry. Carfrae then discovered that physicists had already addressed this problem in some detail. In 1887, mathematician and physicist Lord Kelvin had set himself the task of dividing space into cells of equal volume in the most efficient manner, namely with the lowest possible percentage of surface area interfacing between any two cells. His conjecture, accepted for over a century, was a uniform array of 'tetrakaidecahedra', 14-faced polyhedra, each with six square faces and eight hexagonal faces. Fast forward to 1994, and two brilliant physicists working at Trinity College, Dublin. Professor Denis Weaire and Dr Robert Phelan produced a model that was three per cent more efficient. It comprised two kinds of cells of equal volume: 75 per cent of the cells are tetrakaidecahedra composed of two hexagons and 12 pentagons, and 25 per cent are irregular pentagonal dodecahedra.[19] The supreme efficiency of Weaire-Phelan Foam, whilst not capable of strict proof, has yet to be disputed.

Carfrae's next challenge was that both kinds of foam structure were too regular to be aesthetically

(Opposite) Interior showing the roof of the newly completed railway station at Beijing Capital International Airport Terminal 3.

(Above) Construction workers on the National Stadium, showing details of the structural elements inspired from Chinese-styled 'crazed' pottery.

interesting. His answer was to turn an infinite array of the Weaire-Phelan Foam through an arbitrary angle and then cut the volume of the building—177 by 177 by 32 metres—out of the foam. The resulting faces of the block featured a non-repeating pattern. Spaces for the three major internal volumes and apertures for doors and windows at ground level were hollowed-out from the interior of the block. And the structure would be clad inside and out with ETFE pillows to complete the "desired organic look and to function effectively as an insulated greenhouse". This was Carfrae's 'Eureka!' moment, and an aesthetic triumph. The image of order is fleeting, quickly surpassed by the inescapable appearance of randomness. There is a thrill in this ambiguity between regularity and apparent arbitrariness. It presents a moment to immerse oneself in structured dissolution—or possibly random emergence. But it also prompts the question: "How is this thing arranged?"

After winning the competition, the structure—which until then had not been analysed—needed to be built. The challenges were profound. First, the arbitrary cut through the foam needed to be adjusted so that all the nodes necessary to join the frame were inside the structure. Secondly, for the purposes of the competition design, no element in the structure was repeated. Adjusting the cut through the foam to ensure the nodes were inside the structure also ensured a degree of repetition in the cladding. The result was 4,000 ETFE bubbles, comprising 15 different sizes of bubble in the roof and seven in the walls—some of which span nine metres—which clad the internal and external surfaces. Thirdly, the sheer number of elements required was staggering: 22,000 steel tubes, 12,000 nodes and 4,000 cladding panels. It proved impossible using conventional methods to select the size for each individual structural element which would produce a structure that would stand up. So Arup developed new software that wrapped around and controlled Finite Element Analysis (FEA). This would automatically select the member sizes through an optimisation process. At cycle zero, all 22,000 elements were either overstressed or understressed. For each cycle, every overstressed element would be increased by one step; and every

element less than half-stressed would be reduced by one step. After 25 cycles, the optimally-balanced structure was achieved. The result was ten different sizes of element and four different sizes of spherical node whose distribution could not have been predicted without the help of optimisation software. To indicate just how sensitive the structure is to variation, when doorways were added, the smaller and larger elements changed places. A specially-written script converted the structural analysis wire-frame model into an accurate three-dimensional Computer Aided Design (CAD) model. Construction drawings and schedules were then produced automatically from this three-dimensional model. The system was therefore flexible enough to create a whole new set of construction documents within a week if there were any major changes to the building shape or size during construction.

By happy coincidence, given Beijing's location in a seismic zone, the structure is also highly resistant to earthquakes. It forms a space frame in which all the tubular members are framed into spherical nodes. This simplifies fabrication and ensures that all the members absorb the deforming strains caused by an earthquake, thus making it unlikely that any individual member will fail.[20]

Each ETFE pillow is permanently inflated by a low-power pump, which makes it a better insulator than glass. This helps prevent condensation forming on the interior surface. The 7.2 metre cavity between the ETFE in the ceiling and that covering the roof intensifies the insulative greenhouse effect. Meanwhile, the thermal mass of the pool water and heavyweight surfaces surrounding the pool effectively stores the excess heat during the day and re-emits it at night, minimising variation in thermal load. This enables the whole system to generate an effective negative 'U-value'—the net thermal energy gain to the building. The solar load entering the building offsets its heat losses, leading to an overall saving of around 30 per cent compared to the energy consumption of a standard swimming centre of the same size.

The structure thus meets Ove Arup's ideal of a highly efficient solution, as well as providing the "significant form" and harmonious addition to the environment that Arup urged in his writings and his philosophy—articulated in particular in what is now known within the firm as the "Key Speech".[21] The collaborative nature of the 'Water Cube' project, functional constraints, and the use of structure as a major part of the architectural expression were highly conducive to a close and productive collaboration between engineers and architects on the team. This is what Carfrae did. It is worth emphasising that there were at least 20 members of the interdisciplinary team around the table making collective decisions. This ensured that bad designs were not foisted onto others to deal with. Of course, there were many other aspects to the design of the 'Water Cube' and many roles left unacknowledged here, but the message could not be clearer: an engineer could, and did, undertake the design that played a major part in the aesthetic character of what will be one of the world's most keenly observed buildings.

The 'Water Cube' is low-rise, and its dynamic is sensuously bubble-like. Most of Arup's featured projects in Beijing are powerful structures, whether this is expressed in the understated elegance of Beijing's tallest building, China World Trade Center Phase 3, or the flamboyance of the National Stadium. Certainly, the most imposing of them all is the CCTV building. Together with the adjacent TV Cultural Center (TVCC) it is a high point in 17 years of collaboration between Arup and Rem Koolhaas' Office for Metropolitan Architecture (OMA).[22]

It is perhaps premature to describe it as a culmination, but the completion of the CCTV building marks the realisation of a long-standing research project between Arup and OMA to re-position the global race for ever taller prestige buildings. Thus far, conventional logic dictates that, to produce architecture that is both iconic and high-density, height is the natural solution. However, the race for the sky now looks increasingly absurd, with reports of the Burj Dubai, for example, somewhat neurotically attempting to conceal its vital statistics from imagined rivals. The accolade of 'tallest building in X' is frequently short-lived, as more youthful models breeze into the record books. To avoid succumbing to this preoccupation with stature, a different kind of icon was needed. What is more, functional advantages over its lankier competitors quickly began to emerge.

OMA/Arup's approach has been to explore connected mega-buildings. This found initial expression in un-realised designs for the 'hyper-building' proposed for Bangkok and Universal Studios' headquarters in California.[23] In the CCTV building, the large floor area and connectivity between the towers allow for all the TV station's functions to be carried out in the same building. The ease of circulation amid the towers brings with it the benefit of providing an additional escape route if floors below are hit by fire or other damage. The architects anticipate that the 'loop' arrangement will bring greater interactivity between departments involved in media broadcast, and produce more creative ideas and perhaps encourage new forms of media. To give a sense of the immense scale of the project, the floor space of CCTV is 473,000 square metres; One Canada Square at Canary Wharf in London's Docklands development has 115,000 square metres. The north tower of CCTV is the same height as Canary Wharf at 234 metres, and the whole structure can therefore be thought of as comprising two almost vertical Canary Wharfs joined by two horizontal Canary Wharfs, bent at right angles in the middle, one at the top and one at the bottom.

A night view showing the construction of CCTV, with the China World Trade Center Phase 3, left.

The basic form of the superstructure was devised by Arup in collaboration with OMA. The onus on Arup's engineers was to provide the structural solution. Conventional tall buildings tend to utilise a structural core running up the centre of the building to counteract strong wind loads. Because of the significant overturning forces created by the towers, each of which leans six degrees from the vertical in two directions, creating an incline of ten degrees at the inside corner of each tower, and the overhang—which reaches out 75.2 metres from the north tower and 67.2 metres from the south tower—a sufficiently stiff structural core would be far too large to leave much functional space on most of the floors. As lead engineer of the CCTV project, Rory McGowan points out that we can think of the distribution of the loads in the towers as akin to those in the human leg when the shin is inclined forward and slightly to one side whilst standing, carrying a weight in front to mimic the overhang. To resist the overturning forces and provide enough lateral stability, the engineers suggested perimeter columns of steel-reinforced concrete with bracing, to form a triangulated mesh. The implication of this is threefold. There was a need for incredibly strong and stiff mega columns on the leaning faces of the towers. The use of the word "mega" is frequently bandied about by engineers and architects of big buildings but, in this case, the term appears to be well justified. The columns measure 1.25 by 1.9 metres at the base of the building and contain huge fabricated steel sections embedded within the concrete. They maintain their width all the way to the top of the superstructure, with the depth tapering down to 1.1 metres as the forces reduce. The dimensions are such that they would be capable of supporting a 200-storey conventional tower. The columns on the sloping face, by contrast, carry much less load—equivalent to supporting a conventional 20-storey tower—and are therefore much smaller, with dimensions of 0.6 by 0.9 metres.

Secondly, each tower rests on a solid reinforced concrete raft supported by, respectively, 370 piles that measure 31.5 by 1.2 metres in diameter and 288 piles measuring 33.1 long by 1.2 metres in diameter. Their centres are placed five metres apart. In order to distribute the overturning forces evenly, the centre of each raft is offset from, rather than being beneath, its tower—in the same way that the human foot stabilises the leg as it leans forward. The foundation raft for each tower is therefore 100 by 100 by 7.5 metres deep. The incline of the towers does not put the sloping face into tension, so an 'Achilles tendon', as it were, is not needed. However, some of the piles were designed to take tension should it occur.

The third and most significant aspect of the engineering, with regard to the aesthetics of the CCTV building, is the bracing. Preliminary analysis showed that, when evenly spaced, some parts of the bracing carried much greater loads than others, whereas other parts were redundant. The options were either to strengthen the elements that were under most stress by making them larger, or to increase the number of elements at those points; and in either case remove the elements that were not necessary. The second option was preferred, and the visible result is a densification of the diagonal structural pattern at those points bearing most load, and an opening out of the pattern at those points of least stress. The apparently abrupt endings to some of the densified diagrid elements were seen as an aesthetic virtue by the architects. The absence of a regularly-spaced structure is visually ambiguous, resolved only by an understanding of how the structural engineering works. Kinks in parts of the diagrid can be explained by the combination of functional needs, which necessitate different storey heights and wide access points at ground level, and the structural need for the diagrid members to meet at the joints between the columns and the floorplates every two to three floors in order to act as effective bracing.

The structure represents the most efficient solution for the form of the building, yet it also creates a very striking visual impression, which the architects were keen to preserve. The functional consequences of not having a structural core are also highly significant. Apart from the positioning of the servicing cores, and some corner bracing, the floor plates are left open, to be divisible according to functional needs. This allows for greater flexibility in the future, should those needs change. And, as the architects are quick to point out, media organisations are some of the fastest changing businesses around.

The climactic National Stadium is a more subtle application of Arup engineers' aesthetic skills. Here, the tangled form of the building was envisaged by the artist Ai WeiWei working with the architects Herzog & de Meuron. The challenge for Arup's engineers was to handle the structure sensitively. The result, achieved through the application of CATIA-based software in analysis, realises perfectly the vision of artist and architect, maintaining the visual ambiguity in the structure between primary load-bearing columns and beams and the secondary bracing.[24] 24 primary columns each consist of two outer chords and one inner chord, which emerge from a single point. These chords continue to part from one another as they rise upward before gracefully wrapping over the stands to form the Stadium roof. Each soars at an angle that meets tangentially the elliptical opening, supported by a ten metre-deep truss, before continuing on to the other side of the Stadium and wrapping over the edge to return to the ground via another column. Secondary steelwork triangulates and therefore braces the main structural elements. Careful study will eventually reveal these load-bearing elements, but it is difficult to discern the underlying structure. The eye is constantly drawn by the steel bands weaving all around.

The Beijing Capital International Airport Terminal 3, in contrast to the Stadium's outward structure, was driven by function. There are many aspects to this, four of which are particularly relevant to this text. First, the client wanted plenty of gates to park as many planes as possible onto the edge of the building. This yielded the sweeping concave shape to the sides of the terminal, which maximises the length of the perimeter relative to the floor area of the building, while remaining accessible for aircraft parking. Secondly, because of the scale of the project—at its extremities the building is over three kilometres long and almost 800 metres wide, with a total floor area of over 1.1 million square metres including parking—and because the preliminary design period was just under four months (late November 2003 to late March 2004) with the building opening at the end of February 2008, the structure needed to make use of as many modular parts as possible. Thirdly, roof lights were required to maximise the structure's potential for natural lighting and thermal gain. Arup's engineers ensured that the openings are oriented in such a way to pick up as much of the winter morning sun as possible to heat the building. As the sun rises higher in the sky its rays do not enter the roof lights directly, thereby minimising thermal gain at warmer times of the year, while continuing to provide daylight to the terminal halls below. To facilitate this daylighting, elements of the space frame roof structure were removed beneath the roof lights, thereby producing hexagonal (rather than the standard triangular) openings which are reflected in the patterning of the semi-transparent ceiling. It also produced the asymmetry in the appearance of the roof pattern, since all the roof lights face east: seen from the west, the roof has been likened to dragon's scales glinting in the sun. Arup's lead engineer on the airport Martin Manning confirms this was not part of the design rationale—simply a serendipitous coincidence. And finally, in order to deal with seismic loading, a great deal of attention was paid to the size and detailing of the reinforced concrete and steelwork, notably the giant steel reinforced concrete columns that spring up through the passenger concourses to support the roof.

The design team brought expertise from their experience working together on the London Stansted and Hong Kong Chep Lap Kok airport projects. Central to both projects was a commitment to placing the buildings' ductwork and baggage handling beneath the passenger concourses. The reliance on natural lighting from the glazed facades and roof lights, together with the three-directional diagonally latticed space frame roof structure soaring above, creates a feeling of buoyancy and dynamism. In some respects it is reminiscent of the sense of uplift one feels in cathedrals, only that the proportion of clear glass and relative lack of weighty masonry make it feel still lighter. The semi-transparent ceiling echoes the bamboo rafters of traditional Chinese monumental architecture (seen in the eaves of the Forbidden City, for example), or alternatively of the lightweight bamboo ceilings so typical of houses in southern China. The myriad space truss elements above suggest forest branches—a feeling reinforced by the freshness of the air and the gentle patter of indoor fountains.

In contrast to Tristram Carfrae's contribution to the design of the 'Water Cube', Martin Manning, on T3, is careful to distinguish between his contribution to what he calls architecture with a small 'a' versus that with a big 'A'.

> I'm not sure engineers are [involved in Architecture with a big 'A']. I think what we try to explain is the technical opportunities and the technical problems, and then the Architect with the big 'A' says: "Fine, in that case let's go here." So, whereas we do make a contribution to the way the building is planned, and the shape of the building—in that sense we contributed to the shape—but I will not pretend for a moment that we contributed to the colour or the feeling of space.

Perhaps Manning is right about his own involvement, but it is not clear that having the executive decision-making power of a professional architect is a necessary condition for 'Architectural' influence. The fact that engineers might not make every last suggestion relevant to the final form of a building does not disqualify them from claiming some architectural credit.

While the engineers on each of Arup's projects have played different roles in designing their building's structures, wherever structure determines—rather than merely adapts to—the form or detailing of the building, the engineer is intimately involved in aesthetic as well as structural design. Of course, the process is one of collaboration with architects and artists, and some engineers have been given a wider remit than others to take the initiative when it comes to developing the aesthetic character of their buildings. But engineers should not be coy about this expansive interdisciplinary role. Carfrae describes the collaborative process as akin to an impromptu jam session in which each player will take the creative initiative from time to time, with the architect acting as leader in this metaphorical jazz band. His diagnosis for the direction that design practice is taking is that "computer techniques are used more in the creative process upfront.... The architect [must therefore] become more numerate and the engineer has to become more able to make decisions based on [subjective] judgement, not on absolute fact." The engineer's role is no longer simply to come up with "numbers to justify—say yes or no to—a proposition", but to create some of those design propositions him or herself.

Finally, Manning emphasises that Arup is not about celebrity, that it does not look for its place in history; it simply focuses on solving the client's problems. But, when the clients themselves are seeking a place in history, it is hard not to be propelled towards the collaborative greatness of the result, whether one likes it or not.

1 Quoted in Jencks, Charles, *The Architecture of the Jumping Universe—A Polemic: How Complexity Science Is Changing Architecture and Culture,* Revised Edition, Chichester: Academy Editions, 1997, p. 20.

2 Arup, Ove, "Key Speech", London: Arup, 1970.

3 See Pawley, Martin, "The Rise of the Engineer", reprinted in *The Strange Death of Architectural Criticism: Martin Pawley Collected Writings,* ed. David Jenkins, London: Black Dog Publishing, 2007, pp. 301–303.

4 Saint, Andrew, *Architect and Engineer: A Study in Sibling Rivalry,* London: Yale University Press, 2007, p. 367.

5 Saint, *Architect and Engineer.*

6 The status of High-Tech architecture as 'art' is disputed, even by some of its advocates. Martin Pawley, for example, draws a contrast between a kind of evolutionary approach embodied in High-Tech architecture (which allows for parts of buildings to be added to, dismantled, recycled, or re-used, etc.) and the kind of 'eternal beauty' conception of fine art which confers art status on the basis of aesthetic purity (where the artistic integrity of the piece would be destroyed if anything were added or taken away). See "High-Tech Architecture: History Versus the Parasites", 1991, reprinted in *The Strange Death of Architectural Criticism,* pp. 238–246. Of course, we may argue against this constricted conception of 'art', but it has had significant influence in architectural history.

7 Newby, Frank, "High-Tech or Mys-Tech?", *RIBA Transactions* 6, Vol. 3, no. 2, 1984, p. 22.

8 Saint, *Architect and Engineer,* pp. 383–384.

9 Quoted in Saint, *Architect and Engineer,* p. 386.

10 Quoted in Pawley, "The Secret Life of Engineers", p. 178.

11 Quoted in "Bird's Nest Superstructure", *New Civil Engineer,* 1 January 2007.

12 Ruskin, John, *The Seven Lamps of Architecture,* second edition, [1880], New York: Dover Publications, 1989, II §6, p. 35.

13 Balmond, Cecil, *Informal,* London: Prestel, 2007, pp. 62–64.

14 Balmond, *Informal,* p. 62.

15 Balmond, *Informal,* p. 64.

16 By comparison, Norman Foster's HSBC building in Hong Kong consumes an approximate average of 350 kilograms of steel per square metre.

17 Source: BBC weather online.

18 It is also a curiosity that much of the prefabricated roof cladding on Beijing buildings is either red or blue. This is particularly striking from the air when flying into Beijing or from high up on some of the tall buildings (but can also be seen on Google Maps).

19 "The pressures in these cells are different, so that the interfaces between them have a non-zero constant mean curvature. In both [the Kelvin Foam and the Weaire-Phelan Foam] the cells in the foams meet according to Plateau's rules for soap bubbles: along each singular line, three cells meet at 120 degree angles, and at each vertex, four cells come together tetrahedrally." Brakke, KA & Sullivan, JM "Using Symmetry Features of the Surface Revolver to Study Foams", in HC Hege & K Polthier, eds., *Visualization and Mathematics: Experiments, Simulations and Environments,* New York: Springer-Verlag, 1997 p. 98. (At the same time that Kelvin was dividing space efficiently, Plateau was determining the geometry of soap bubbles.)

20 Seismic stresses can be lateral (in either direction), vertical, or torsional. Carfrae describes the Water Cube structure as a "damp cushion" which can stretch in 44,000 different locations simultaneously in order to absorb earthquake energy. Not only is the structure incredibly flexible, it could also be attached to the face of a cliff by [any] of its sides and not sheer.

21 Arup, "Key Speech", p. 1.

22 It is also worth noting that the long-term collaboration between Arup and OMA has been so successful that a significant number of young designers at OMA who have gone on to form their own architectural practices (such as Dutch firm MVRDV and London-based Foreign Office Architects) have since teamed up with Arup on many of their projects.

23 See Koolhaas, Rem, et al, *Content,* London: Taschen, 2004, pp. 422–425.

24 CATIA (Computer Aided Three-dimensional Interactive Application) software was developed for the aerospace and automotive industries and is now gaining popularity in the world of architectural design because of its capability to design and analyse structural (and cladding) elements that curve in multiple directions.

PROJECT BEIJING: TIME, SCALE, TRANSFORMATION

VESNA PETRESIN ROBERT

PROJECT BEIJING: TIME, SCALE, TRANSFORMATION

TRANSFORMING BEIJING

The stratospheric rate of construction taking place in today's Beijing is a clear sign of the city's newly rediscovered vitality. This formerly solemn fortress of Socialism has become emboldened with a fresh idealism that makes the Chinese capital one of the world's architectural hotspots. The unique synergy of the challenging projects taking shape today in the Asian metropolis—and described elsewhere in this book—comes as the country opens its doors to the world and enjoys a booming, if idiosyncratic, market economy. With an increase in density needed to counterbalance the rising property prices—along with more efficient land use—Beijing's planning authorities have boldly invested in a major rebuilding of the city. The resulting projects that have emerged on such a gargantuan scale are aimed at a total re-branding of the city and, symbolically, the country it represents.

THE TWENTY-FIRST CENTURY METROPOLIS: A BAROMETER OF SOCIAL AND ECONOMIC TRENDS

Although China has one of the world's most ancient cultures, it is only within the past century that the country has witnessed its most dramatic period of economic growth and urbanisation. In this relatively short period of time, Chinese society quickly progressed from being feudal to colonial, only to then become a Communist state, and ultimately moving towards a market economy in the information age.

The complexity that characterises many contemporary cities has long been part of Beijing's pedigree. As early as the Ming period, the Chinese capital was arranged in a tightly interwoven urban sequence, with residential, shopping, governmental and religious spaces coming together to create a complicated mix that would leave many of our most modern urbanites disoriented.

Today, China's urban environment is being reshaped once more, as it experiences an unprecedented rate of urban, economic, social, technological and ecological change. Whether such explosive growth brings better lifestyles or creates increasingly harsh living and working conditions remains an open question. Deyan Sudjic, Director of London's Design Museum and a prominent commentator on design trends, describes this vortex of changes in his article "Cities on the edge of chaos":

> The dispossessed and the ambitious are flooding into cities swollen out of all recognition. Poor cities are struggling to cope. Rich cities are reconfiguring themselves at breakneck speed. China has created an industrial power house from what were fishing villages in the 1970s.[1]

Changes in urban lifestyles and the dramatic rise of environmental issues are triggering a number of trends in contemporary cities worldwide. For a city such as Beijing, this takes the form of new urban structures to respond to demographic pressures; building by incorporating elements of nature—less from an aesthetic perspective than from a sustainability perspective; urbanisation by implementing advanced modern infrastructure; and the recycling of pre-existing urban fabric. And what has also become clear, in Beijing's version of the twenty-first century metropolis, is that iconic buildings have become major tools for city branding.

Such a fast-paced transformation of urban and social structure also calls for a fresh perspective. Complex urban structures require a design strategy that reflects the dynamics of urban growth and decay, and which includes the all-important networks of transportation and communication. Change is an unavoidable constant.

Today, there are more cities on the planet that are larger than ever in recorded history. In the nineteenth century, an estimated ten per cent of the population lived in cities. By 2008, the proportion had increased to over 50 per cent. And with the majority of today's urban population to be found in emergent economies, it is not surprising that any trends-forecasting is predominantly city-oriented.

Growing networks have also induced the phenomenon of urban growth as a sprawl. To prevent it, Beijing expanded and densified its infrastructure, most recently with the transformation of its public transport infrastructure, including a new international terminal at the Beijing Capital International Airport and the creation of a major transport hub at Beijing South Rail Station. At the same time, the city has increased its internet connectivity, bolstering its communications networks.

Cities tend to develop by responding to the unpredictable dynamics of the market and society—and not necessarily in the ways dreamed up by their planners. In today's hybrid metropolis, form is a result of feedback information. As in nature, complex urban behaviour emerges from the capacity for self-organising. Architects and designers are no longer the only ones determining functional and symbolic aspects of space. This role is increasingly being taken over by engineers—and software developers.

ARUP: A GLOBAL 'KNOWLEDGE NETWORK'

Arup is the firm of designers, engineers and business consultants that has been the creative force behind many of the world's most innovative and sustainable buildings, transport and civil engineering projects.

Artist's impression of the Beijing South Rail Station viewed from the west.

It has worked in China since 1976, where almost a quarter of Arup's 10,000-strong worldwide staff now work.

The firm has worked on over 500 projects in China, including sports venues, masterplans, hotels, airports, cultural venues, financial centres, embassies, media headquarters, power stations, bridges, motorways and railways.

China's rapid development presents both a challenge and an opportunity to a firm such as Arup, with its strong principle of investing in people: offices in Hong Kong and mainland China recruit students from local universities to bring new talent into the firm. Hundreds of professional engineers have been trained and over 300 graduates recruited in the last ten years. Developing local leadership is one of the priorities. Combined with a promotion of the transfer of knowledge and know-how, Arup makes significant contributions to the development of the built environment and the design profession in China.

The company was founded in 1946 by Sir Ove Arup, the visionary Danish philosopher and engineer. He founded it on the concept of "total architecture", emphasising the importance of holistic design and collaboration between people in order to achieve the best result.

This approach is still taken in the firm today, and can be seen in the way that it has tackled the many projects on view today in Beijing.

Steven Burrows, a director at Arup and one of the people responsible for the firm's sport activities, is the stadium expert who led the engineering of the complex National Stadium nicknamed the 'Bird's Nest', in Beijing. He uses the example of stadium design to explain how Arup's philosophy is key to the successful delivery of complex designs in Beijing, one of the world's most demanding emergent markets:

> There are about 42 different disciplines required to deliver a stadium—there is certainly nobody in the local geography who has done it before and there are not many people in the world who have got experience that they can take from geography to geography. So it seemed a perfect vehicle for Arup as we have all these skills in-house; we operate in a lot of places around the world, and we are a sharing company that does not have local profit centres. We bring in all the experts to deliver every single project. Arup's multi-disciplinary capability is unmatched. There are no other engineering and design firms that provide a complete top to bottom service for a stadium. We have stadium architects and designers, and even have turf specialists in Australia, acousticians that specialise in stadium acoustics, and sports lighting experts. That gives us a unique position in our market.[2]

The train station connecting Beijing Capital International Airport Terminal 3 to the city.

ORIGINS OF THE BEIJING UTOPIA

China today represents a test-bed for progressive design. It offers a new freedom to build in a way that many Western societies have not experienced since post-war development. But can design still successfully drive 'fast-forward' urban transformations, or have lessons from historic utopias shown us new ways of sustainable urban development?

Many of the most ambitious planning experiments are happening in China, including sustainable new cities. Consider also the rapid urbanisation of a place such as Shenzhen, which has grown from a fishing village to a metropolis of 13 million inhabitants in just 28 years. While cities in Europe evolved over centuries, many of China's largest cities have been created within the past few decades. Nowhere else in the world have cities developed at such a merciless pace. Unsurprisingly, the speed of urbanisation raises questions about life-cycles and sustainability.

And, in this case, rebuilding Beijing for the twenty-first century may well turn out to be the successful combination of an uncompromising utopia with the boldness of a high-speed market-driven need, with the delivery of projects that range from landmark buildings to transport infrastructure.

Throughout history, there are many examples of how utopian models of place creation, set in an ideal world with few constraints, have influenced urban designers. In Renaissance Italy, the concept of an 'Ideal City', notably Filarete's 'Sforzinda', influenced the radial, star-shaped, centralised planning of city-states such as Ferrara and Palmanova.[3]

But the value of such utopias—a term first popularised by Sir Thomas More's 1515 novel *Utopia*—can be ambiguous: their implicit perfection also indicates a futile expectation for a better future.[4]

The utopia of Beijing is embodied early in the Ming capital, Dadu, its perfectly-ordered layout described in the classical Confucian text *Zhou Li—The Rites of Zhou*, as an ideal city, and probably realised in Khubilai's summer retreat, referred to as the "Xanadu" in Samuel Taylor Coleridge's poem.[5]

The plan for this ideal city revealed the ability of Chinese civilisation to organise and deliver construction work—or any mobilisation of people for that matter—on a large scale in a very short time-frame. Grandiose projects such as the Great Wall and the First Emperor's capital and tomb near modern Xi'an (which houses his third century BC terra-cotta army), as well as the sixth century Grand Canal, further demonstrate that emperors have never hesitated to uproot populations in great numbers.

History shows that blindly-embraced utopias typically end up falling apart. Ironically, in the twenty-first century, virtual urbanisms, like those of Second Life, suffer from similar design and social issues and potential planning traps, while their correlation with physical urban developments and organisation processes is becoming increasingly important.

Utopian towns were never truly global, but rather, like the ideal city of Palmanova in Italy, were small and clearly legible; they have never greatly challenged social and moral conventions, or considered the possibility for any of their residents to exist anonymously. Note that utopias of larger cities developed only after the Industrial Revolution: garden towns that connected smaller urban units together were conceived to contrast with large agglomerations, creating communities rather than urban societies. Reactions against mass-urban society continued in the utopias of the 1960s: Marshall McLuhan's "Global Village" statement was a metaphor—and not a particularly positive one at that—for a society whose success was based on electronic means of communication in a thoroughly connected world.[6]

One of the boldest utopias was expressed in the Charter of Athens, drawn up in 1933 on a Mediterranean cruise by the pioneers of Modernist architecture.[7] While it initially proposed an ideal modern city divided into functional zones, organised to maximise the use of space and sunlight, it later degenerated into ruthless mass-urbanisation with unsustainable building materials and an absence of human scale. The Modern Movement, branded the "International Style" in 1932 by Alfred H Barr Jr, the Director of The Museum of Modern Art, was in essence a utopian movement aiming to address the challenges of an industrialised urban environment by means of architecture. This extended to the artistic and political realms, as befitted the new modern era of egalitarian and participatory democracies, and was a movement filled with euphoria and optimism. Peter Blake claims that architecture, which had always served the elite, had the opportunity to remake the world that had been devastated by war in Europe and which had been constrained by severe economic conditions in the United States.[8] Aesthetically, it represented a reaction against the Neoclassical style often favoured by totalitarian regimes of the time. The modernist utopia was brought down when postmodernism introduced the idea of cities based on a bottom-up approach—namely chaotic and reflecting diversity—rather than being planned to reflect the image of society, as Venturi argued in his *Complexity and Contradiction in Architecture*.[9]

In the same period and on the other side of the globe, China was experiencing its own version of modernism, sometimes referred to as "Third World Modernism". It was a mass-utopia that amplified the numerous contradictions of its Western counterpart.

Inspired by the Russian utopian revolution of the early twentieth century, Third World Modernism was rooted in the notion of the ideal world, one that had not yet arrived. But unlike Communism, where utopia was an end-goal, the Third World Modernism propelled utopia as a process, creating expectations of a world that would exist once people freed themselves from the constraints of reality, most notably colonial rule.

In 1958, the "Great Leap Forward" was announced by the National People's Congress. Modernity became entwined in a complex relationship between goals of revolution and development, with the past being seen as an obstacle to the realisation of a perfect future. Modernism, denoting a belief in progress through technology and science, was the mantra espoused by the state that drove these utopian-yet-authoritarian large-scale transformations of lifestyles that would lead to a new social order. The phenomenon of communes instrumentalised these utopian aspirations, as the academic Duanfang Lu comments:

> The Chinese People's Commune movement can be looked at as a concrete manifestation of the high modernist vision. Built on fantasies of industrial and social modernity, commune modernism was directed by a faith in the possibility of overcoming the past to create a brand new world. Like many high modernist experiments in other parts of the world, however, the mass utopia only left a history of disasters in its wake.[10]

In the 1980s, the government created "Special Economic Zones" to test the effects of a free market economy on China. This allowed new forms of utopian urbanisation—such as Shenzhen—to be developed. The success of these zones allowed the socialist system to adapt and to embrace a new economic model that was closer to the traditional Chinese spirit of entrepreneurship.

In the post-Mao period, Chinese industry moved out of the city into designated development zones, which allowed large plots of land within the city to be redeveloped. Many old buildings were demolished to make way for a new urban matrix of transport, infrastructure, retail facilities, office headquarters and leisure spaces. But rather than making reference to the visions of its past, the Beijing of today is a blank canvas on which the country's new quasi-capitalist economic vision can be projected. Experimental and utopian developments are being encouraged, but the city is still trying to shape its national and architectural identity.

It is the contrasting forces of high-cost lifestyles and low-cost workers, the faith in the power of real estate and a focus on finance, technology, logistics and culture that make up contemporary Beijing. Secondary industries are giving way to tertiary industries; manufacturing is being replaced with culture. In this fast-growing metropolis, design is an instrument for encouraging economic growth.

Chinese cities are living laboratories, constantly changing and evolving. Their value lies in their constant creation of new meanings. Justin McGuirk, a commentator on these developments, sees Shenzhen as symptomatic for Chinese urban growth: it is an urban as well as socio-economic experiment, promoting the national ethos of growth and regeneration.[11]

RECYCLING BEIJING

Beijing has found itself in a cycle of demolition and reconstruction for centuries, but the short-term political effects that urban re-branding brings often leave behind a number of issues, such as the value of historic buildings and enterprises, or a trail of "Junkspace", as architect Rem Koolhaas calls structures past their sell-by date.[12] The drive to modernise space and society often overwhelms the preservation of traditional structures, although paradoxically, the historic importance of the location is immensely valued.

Beijing has recruited an astonishing number of labourers to build its new landmarks. But this should not be viewed as something new. Throughout their history, the Chinese have demonstrated the ability to instantly organise large numbers of labourers on mega-structures. When the Song dynasty (916–1234) retreated to Hangzhou after the Mongolian invasion in 1126, the new rulers recycled the building material from the buildings in Kaifeng, the former Northern Song capital, report authors Li, Dray-Novey and Kong:

> A workforce of 800,000 men and 400,000 troops used these architectural fragments to create the Jin palace at Zhongdu, appropriating not only Kaifeng's debris but also its technical diagrams and human resources, its skilled artisans, and drew upon ongoing advances in Chinese technology, especially in hydraulic engineering.[13]

The symmetrical layout of the capital, together with the ability to recruit a workforce instantly, expressed the inherent centralism of the country's politics and culture. Architecture was used to display power.

The origins of the twenty-first century construction boom taking place today in Beijing are more probably rooted in the frenetic construction of the 1950s and 60s that assisted the shaping of a new, Socialist society. Then, the Beijing city walls were torn down along with traditional lifestyles and aesthetics. The current construction has swept away many *hutongs*, the treasured traditional dwellings and narrow alleyways, but has raised buildings that have the potential to outperform any development in the West.

However, the rash of euphoric construction has inevitably brought along a certain amount of unsophisticated detailing, planning or commercial development, which has made many Chinese suspect that the old might have been unnecessarily sacrificed for the new, 'un-Chinese', architecture. However, as one Chinese proverb sums up: "If the old doesn't go, the new won't come."

AUTHENTICITY VERSUS NOVELTY

Rem Koolhaas, of OMA, and co-designer of the China Central Television Headquarters in Beijing, confronts the crux of the Chinese architectural dilemma:

> The Chinese city is for me a city that has built up a lot of volume in a very short time, which therefore doesn't have the slowness that is a condition for a traditional sedimentation of a city, which for us is still the model for authenticity. Beyond a certain speed of construction that kind of authenticity is inevitably sacrificed, even if you build everything out of stone and authentic materials, and that's a kind of irony. There is no escaping the artificial in the new architecture, and certainly not in large amounts of architecture being generated at the same time.[14]

Buckminster Fuller famously remarked that we can never change things by fighting the existing reality.

An evening view of the China World Trade Center Phase 3 under construction. Cranes are silhouetted at the tower's summit.

Rather, to change something, we should build a new model that makes the existing model obsolete. Therefore, to set conditions that allow innovation means allowing a creative process that leads to a successful exploitation of new ideas in any setting. In the international, multi-disciplinary setting in which the new Beijing architecture is taking shape, innovation is a vital ingredient for competitiveness, productivity, and social gain. Brand expert Ralph Ardill notes that:

> Once you've worked on a truly innovative project, you realise how important transformation is to the success or failure of a project. Your way of thinking changes, your priorities change, your company changes and your way of working changes forever. True innovation is not just about changing a product, a service or even a marketplace; it is also about recognising and relishing the need to change yourself.[15]

For Arup's engineers, innovation already takes place at the early stages of conceptualising a building's structure. Benefits include flexibility and transparency in design collaboration, project management, as well as lower costs and optimisation of structure. With such conditions, design excellence and sustainable infrastructure can work their way beyond mere slogans and become organically-integrated building principles.

From a Chinese perspective, innovation in design stands for problem-solving the unpredictable and multiple sets of constraints. As China seeks its own new form of modernity at a time of globalisation, choices must be made between following and appropriating the Western position, or finding originality in an alternative relationship to information, technology and urban development.

A growing number of young and talented Chinese designers and architects are producing works that merge individuality with an awareness of the country's rich historic heritage, as well as the latest international trends. This might be the path to an original Chinese architecture, and possibly even a model for cultures in other emergent economies.

CULTIVATING COLLABORATION

China today is trying to change its image and regain the pride of a culture that gave the world ink, gunpowder, pagoda roofs, screens, joints, and architectural feats like the Great Wall. It was indeed as early as the Song dynasty that the Chinese began fostering intellectual and creative collaboration.

Further examples exist of a spirit of collaboration that grew organically throughout Chinese history, and which also included the practice of having monumental architecture designed 'offshore'.

Under the rule of the Mongol empire, the splendour of the country's capital—then called Yuan Dadu, with its innovative architecture of the highest standard—was a direct result of an extraordinary cultural collaboration. In their book *Beijing*, the authors Li, Drey-Novey and Kong report that, although its builders were Chinese, the design ideas were contributed by Persian and Arab mathematicians and engineers as much as by Chinese scholars.[16] The architects of Dadu were *Yeheidie'er*, a Muslim family of Asian origin who carried out the designs under supervision of the Han Chinese, with Muslim, Persian, Khitan and Jurchen artisans that the Khan Khubilai drew from his vast empire. Merchants came to the picturesque markets of Dadu from Russia, Central Asia, Persia and Northern India. Even Western Europeans, of whom Marco Polo is perhaps the most famous example, were coming to live in the crowded, vibrant capital. Li, Dray-Novey and Kong explain:

> It was not the last time in Chinese history that a dynasty of Inner Asian origin would tap the skills

> of people from many lands to enhance its image and power. This pattern would recur under the last dynasty, the Qing, when eighteenth century Jesuit architects would contribute to imperial court capabilities and especially to the design of part of a summer palace. Throughout its existence as a capital, Beijing has been molded by both Chinese and non-Chinese influences.[17]

In the thirteenth century, Marco Polo reports of the capital of China whose wealth and impressive scale far exceeded the achievements of late Medieval Europe.

In the sixteenth century, another Italian, the Jesuit missionary Matteo Ricci, 1552–1610, lived in China. He learned the language and was supported by the Ming elite to write, in collaboration with Chinese scholars, books on astronomy, mathematics, cartography, geography, medicine, ethics and linguistics. Furthermore, Jesuits helped improve the knowledge of space, geometry and optics at the Qing court, cultivating painting, cartography and architecture. The dynasty was known to commission works from foreign artists and craftsmen.

During the rule of the last emperors, translations of major Western works into Chinese took place assisted by Presbyterian missionaries, including subjects such as international law, political economy, natural philosophy, history, anatomy and physical geography. New modern-style academies were founded for boys and girls, teaching science and languages as well as Chinese and Christian philosophy.

The 1920s and 30s brought a fascination with Western architectural styles, but foreign intellectuals were equally drawn to the dynamic capital of the Republic of China. Bertrand Russell, the famous British philosopher, lived in China for a year, lecturing on economic, social and educational reforms. But the modernisation of Beijing also brought resistance to new construction, which was considered by many Chinese architects as a foreign intrusion, disrupting the aesthetic harmony of the capital.

This makes it all the more significant that the Beijing government has actively chosen to collaborate with Western architects and designers. Creating the new twenty-first century Beijing accentuates once again the city's international, contemporary aspect. However, there is a fine line between modernising and destroying the old. The French architect, Paul Andreu, who designed the National Theatre in Beijing, notoriously refused to conform to the traditional values of the city, such as its symmetry: "I would like to add a new chapter to this history, which is to cut off from history. For the sake of preserving an ancient culture, the best way is to push it towards a margin of crisis".[18]

What was perceived by most Chinese as arrogance was considered by the Beijing authorities as the first and necessary step to break away from the past and allow further futuristic, avant-garde architecture to be built at later stages.

The most interesting characteristic of collaboration on building the new Beijing is probably a close interaction of architects and engineers, developers and leaders. Teams working on the Chinese Central Television's headquarters (designed by Arup and OMA), the National Stadium (designed by Arup, Herzog & de Meuron, and the Beijing Design Institute CAG) and the National Aquatics Center (Arup, PTW and CCDI), observed that none of the developers and policy-makers seemed older than 45. While the young generation of Chinese architects are gaining the experience to design and manage grand construction projects, high profile architectural names such as Rem Koolhaas, Herzog & de Meuron, Norman Foster, and Terry Farrell were the ones to bring international prestige to Beijing.

And although the Beijing of the 1980s and 90s may have favoured the commercial aesthetics of retail buildings, tastes have evolved, and so has China's socio-economic position.

From the perspective of Western architects, China now offers an incomparable opportunity to create ambitious architectural landmarks—despite the country's bureaucratic complexities. As foreign design firms are legally not allowed to do the complete design of a building, and as contractors are state-controlled agencies, collaboration with local firms is a necessity. To make matters even more interesting, building regulations are often restrictive and not in tune with international standards, and a low-cost approach to the detailing stage often endangers the brilliance of the overall design concept. However, close collaboration between Chinese clients, design institutes and Western architects and engineers can—and often does—initiate a new, authentic Chinese contemporary style. Through this relationship, Western designers can learn a lot from the traditional Chinese view on the relationship between man and nature, and young Chinese practices can gain experience in the latest building techniques.

With this new openness from China to the global market comes a new sense of national identity and design, and young students of architecture and engineering in China are taking inspiration from the international design scene.

Learning first-hand from the architects and engineers building the twenty-first century Beijing will revolutionise the domestic knowledge-base, and in this sense, Arup's influence extends more widely than simply through its engineering design and planning. The firm's active encouragement of the transfer of knowledge is creating major opportunities in Beijing for a new generation of Chinese designers and engineers.

Craig Gibbons, a Director at Arup and project manager for the new headquarters of CCTV, comments:

> Normally in China, tenders of contracts the size as large as the Olympic projects are routinely assessed. In our project for CCTV, of the three short-listed tenderers [for the contract to build the iconic structure], each one wanted to approach construction in a different way. This was interesting as, prior to that, the client had wanted us to describe exactly the sequence in which the CCTV should be built. I suggested we make it a little more open-ended. With complex buildings, contractors are given the freedom to explore different approaches. In the case of CCTV, where the two cantilevering elements have to be joined in a single point, I envisaged incrementally cantilevering out the overhang, or building it up on the ground floor, then jacking it into position, or building a temporary tower under the overhang and then constructing the overhang hanging off it. It was interesting that out of the three short-listed tenderers, one of them chose to do it by cantilever, another one to build it on the ground, and the last one chose to do a temporary tower. There are different ways of building, and as designers we have to anticipate that and also make sure that the contractors are given the freedom to explore these opportunities.[19]

Michael Kwok, a Director at Arup who runs the firm's business in China, explains:

> The way of working in China in terms of foreign designers, whether you are an architect or engineer, is to work with a local partner; these are authorised companies, so you have to make sure that you work well together. Arup has been around for a while in China, and therefore the communication with the locals was not an issue because we understand the culture and the ways of working.
>
> It was interesting to work with a different designer in China on each project. How we actually come together to work with a particular designer involves a lot of factors. A particular local design firm may be

A view of the CCTV construction site with the TVCC building to the right.

recommended by the client. Then there are occasions when we are invited by the architects. We also have a working relationship with a particular local design partner, and there are also cases where we know a particular local design company that we like to work with, so we invite them into the team. There are different situations in different projects. But all in all, we find that everybody has been supportive of Arup's work.[20]

Gibbons stresses the collaborative processes involved in designing and building the monumental CCTV:

It was very much a true collaboration. Rory McGowan, together with Chris Carroll and his team in London, were the key players in the development of the form of building. One of the most galling issues was that designer buildings in China—and particularly in Beijing, where it is very seismic—have to follow the rules about conformity of shape, spacing of columns, and height of building for those structural systems. That probably explains why architecture in China, up until recent times, all looked very similar: it had to, in order to be built! But when our scheme was developed it broke every single rule about how buildings should be built—certainly in China, but probably in other parts of the world as well. The form of the building was basically completely non-compliant with the many constraints within the Chinese code. It was one of those thought-provoking moments. When the client asked us whether we could build the structure, our answer was invariably affirmative; but a structure like the one for CCTV had never been attempted before, and we had been facing very restrictive procedures, requiring us to comply with codes that were not really applicable. There was a lot of discussion at Arup in the early

> stages to actually look at what would be required to deliver such a project. We had to push the boundaries—not challenge the authorities, but rather rewrite the rulebook in order to deliver this iconic design.[21]

THE CHANGING ROLE OF THE ENGINEER AND ARCHITECT

With the spectacularly designed and brilliantly engineered projects for the new Beijing, Arup has established itself as a paragon of progressive achievement—a collaborative entity that combines cutting-edge design with humanistic principles. The boundary between architect and engineer is blurring once again, and a mutual interdependence can be detected in the work on display in Beijing—with collaboration in many cases becoming very much like a design workshop.

This tallies with Arup's long-standing support of architecture, transforming the ideas of architects into reality. Tristram Carfrae, a principal of Arup in Australia and designer of the 'Water Cube' in Beijing, explains that the era of architects as the sole authors of a building is coming to a close, and that the creative powers of engineering are just as important in contributing to a work of architecture—which is ultimately a team effort.

Similarly, Steven Burrows comments:

> In the case of a complex geometry of a building, you can envisage a situation where if the architect changes the geometry of a building, the engineering changes entirely as well. This results in repeated re-designing, which is not great use of the client's money. Our view is that the engineer should partner with the architect, which would result in fewer fundamental design changes and which would allow us all to control costs. In this sense, engineering does not follow architecture but rather becomes an equal partner in design. The design changes might not occur so often because good engineering decisions have been made at the start. In an office block, for example, the structural content of an office block is between about 20–25 per cent of the cost of the building. In the case of a stadium, the structural content will be at least 50 per cent of the stadium cost. This simple metric shows you why it is even more important for architecture and engineering to work in harmony on a complex project such as a stadium, than perhaps it is on an office development.[22]

According to Cecil Balmond, one of Arup's foremost designers and former Deputy Chairman of Arup, structural engineering is becoming more about explorations of form and geometry, and about complexity, reflecting the ambiguity in modern-day life. He believes that the accepted Cartesian world is merely a subset of a more complex existence. Therefore, architects may need to engage with creative principles of engineering to create inventive solutions, especially as engineering disciplines are usually assigned two-thirds of a building's budget. The rapid advance of technology is another important driver of change, introducing new materials, translating them into new forms and architectural typologies—whether they be virtual, material or hybrid. Architects today engage with the knowledge of a multitude of disciplines, linking the insights of scientists, artists, craftsmen, philosophers and entrepreneurs.

Cecil Balmond, one of the engineers behind the structural concept of CCTV, also designs, builds, writes, sculpts and exhibits to draw attention to the fact that buildings today are no longer static, but are dynamic and responsive to the environment and their users.

ARUP: AN INSPIRATION FOR EMERGING CHINESE ARCHITECTURE

Arup's role in helping to shape the new cosmopolitan Beijing is vital: here is a city where architecture is

A view of the 'Bird's Nest' structure during construction.

a driver of economic growth and urban identity, and where urban regeneration provides significant opportunities for ambitious designers.

In the 1990s, Europe went through its own dramatic political, economic and social changes with the fall of the Communist regimes. Regions and borders that had been erased by the former Soviet Bloc began to re-emerge, former continental metropolises were revitalised, and new centres of urban and political power were established. With a decline in the importance of industrialisation as a stimulus for growth—together with the rise of the information revolution—there were economic as well as cultural transformations. Old city cores were regenerated, new bypass roads promoted traffic flow, and landmark buildings were inserted as design statements to attract attention, investment and talent. Spectacles such as the Olympic Games stimulated the infrastructural renewal of Barcelona, the World Fair (Expo) allowed regeneration of Seville and Lisbon, and cultural revitalisation brought iconic buildings, mainly in the form of museums, to cities such as Bilbao, Paris and Berlin. European cities in the 1990s went through a process of re-branding and city marketing, making full use of the iconic creations of international star architects.

But compared with Europe, or even emerging economic forces such as India or Dubai, the scale of Beijing's urban transformation is gargantuan; the metropolis is changing at an unprecedented rate. Through its work in the capital, Arup is contributing to what might be termed a 'renaissance' of Chinese architecture.

Many young architects in China have been learning from the process of modernising and constructing the new Beijing. They are developing a fresh, intelligent and specific style of design that is uniquely Chinese and breaks away from the past ideology that often disposed of the historic qualities of Chinese towns.

The two leaning towers of CCTV are at a precarious ten degree angle towards each other.

The phenomenon of the Beijing boom may also be attributed to a reform programme in the 1980s when Beijing shifted from its role as an industrial city to a political, cultural, scientific and technological centre. Li, Dray-Novey and Kong report in *Beijing* that this raised questions about Chinese history and culture, the environmental dangers of rapid urban expansion, as well as a commitment to progress in construction, transport infrastructure, tourism and heritage.[23]

The economic rebirth of China has been further accelerated by a new ideology of personal freedom and direct expression. Globalisation and the electronic communications revolution redefined Beijing and changed its inhabitants' lifestyles, but the growing consumerism also brought an uncritical demolition of the traditional way of living, a plethora of high-rise buildings and large retail complexes, traffic congestion and pollution. The city has once again become trapped in the complex conflict between urban modernisation and historic tradition, although it has also become more fluid and accessible to a migrant workforce, entrepreneurs and artists.

Rory McGowan of Arup, one of the project Directors for the CCTV building, explains:

> China is changing—its commerce, business income, control of the workforce and lifestyle has loosened up. Comparing a standard news-stand in a Beijing street today to even five years ago tells us everything—the number of publications available now is incredible.
>
> It is extraordinary to have five world-class architects working in Beijing. The building that will have the longest fall-out by far is the CCTV headquarters. It is without parallel and I neither see it as a Chinese project, nor do I see it as a Beijing project, or a central business district project, but rather as an international one. It questions the future of density in cities, and the slavish admiration of skyscrapers with a single

> method of circulation—up and down. CCTV is going to be a debating point in building design for decades.[24]

THE ART OF COMPETITION

The cutting-edge projects for the New Beijing—the most visible ones being the new headquarters of CCTV, the National Aquatics Center, Beijing Capital International Airport Terminal 3 and the National Stadium—go hand in hand with an urban experiment, following relaxation of property regulations. New buildings for the public include transport, health, sport, entertainment, and mass-communication, and address the key requirements of a twenty-first century metropolis.

But while many local architects and critics have reservations about these designs—they have been described as alien, expensive and making the city unrecognisable—most welcome the fresh ideas that the 2008 Olympic Games and the associated stimulus for new buildings that it has brought to Beijing.

It is worth remembering that before Pierre de Coubertin revived the Olympic Movement and organised the first Modern Olympic Games in 1900, the original Olympic Games of Ancient Greece—which were held in the years between 776 BC–393 AD—represented a way of resolving political tensions with sports as the catalyst.[25] Wars between the city-states, the *polis*, were halted: the mission of the Games was to unite people through physical endeavour, rather than divide them through territorial interests.

Michael Kwok explains the significance of the Olympic Movement to Beijing:

> The Olympics is one of the catalysts for what is happening in Beijing at the moment. Of all the projects [be they commercial, residential buildings, for example], the Olympics play a major part because the infrastructure obviously needs to be improved for the Games to take place. Beijing wants to use the Olympics to sell its new face and show the world that China can host a major international event, but also demonstrate a positive change that such an event can bring to the city. Olympic buildings in Beijing may not be the most cost-effective structures for a particular programme such as a stadium, but we have to recognise that they are now becoming the new icons of the city. Beijing, of course, has its own historic icons that have been major tourist attractions, but I believe it needs something new and stimulating that attracts both international visitors and is appreciated by the locals.[26]

The new designs that Arup has collaborated on with acclaimed Western architects and Chinese design institutes are ground-breaking in every respect: the ambitious National Stadium, where up to 7,000 construction workers would gather on the site on any day, is an iconic design with a steel frame and a 91,000-seat arena. After the Olympics, this area will be landscaped and, as Jonathan Glancey, Architecture and Design Editor of *The Guardian* newspaper hopes, "the Olympic Park might yet turn out to be an 'Unforbidden City', a people's palace gardens of the future".[27]

The National Aquatics Center features an innovative structural form based upon the way that soap bubbles join together to fill space, and making use of innovative cladding, creates a bubble-like appearance.

The expansion of Beijing Capital International Airport via the futuristic Terminal 3 building has been engineered by Arup with Norman Foster, and will have the capacity of over 80 million passengers per year

The Beijing South Rail Station, by Arup and Terry Farrell and Partners, has a striking design that

The roof structure of the train station at Beijing Capital International Airport Terminal 3.

is strongly reminiscent of traditional Chinese architecture and a roof form that pays homage to the Hall for Prayer for Good Harvests in Beijing's Temple of Heaven. This oval structure measuring 500 by 380 metres, is also one of the world's largest catenary roof structures.

The new headquarters of CCTV, designed by Arup with the pioneering firm of architects, OMA, is an unconventional, 234 metre high trapezoidal, continuously-looping structure of interlinked towers, with 473,000 square metres of space for broadcasting studios, offices, hotels and exhibition areas. The designers from OMA had to soften the Beijing planners' conservative attitude (no doubt due, in part, to being located in a high-risk seismic zone) to enable the construction of such a radical project. It is unlikely that a building of such a form and scale could be built anywhere else in the world at this moment in time. Rem Koolhaas of OMA explains it best in his "Beijing Manifesto":

> In early 2002, my office received two invitations: one to propose a design for Ground Zero, the other to propose a design for the headquarters of China Central Television in Beijing. We discussed the choice over Chinese food. The life of the architect is so fraught with uncertainty and dilemmas that any clarification of the future, including astrology, is disproportionately welcome. My fortune cookie that night read: "Stunningly Omnipresent Masters make minced meat of memory". We chose China.[28]

As Beijing increases its number of new, cutting-edge buildings almost in real-time, it is worth reflecting that such epochal transformations may also indicate that this billion-strong nation is not entering modernity as much as it is leaping directly to the frontiers of postmodernity.

A view of the overhang of the CCTV building, with the China World Trade Center Phase 3 in the distance.

CREATING URBAN FUTURES

The significance of Arup's leading role in the regeneration of China, and the city of Beijing in particular, may lie in a successful partnership between local skills and opportunities on one hand, and Arup's global knowledge network on the other. Arup's pioneering role in enabling design excellence and fostering successful creative design partnerships represents a way of working from which China could start building its own modern legacy.

After an initial phase of bold and rapid development with buildings serving as corporate images, Chinese architecture may now be in a position to focus on subtlety and substance. Younger architects have already found their link with the Chinese tradition of invention, and in transforming the old conventions. Their work focuses on issues of materiality and construction; they seek to innovate in the context of a tight budget and local environment. Rather than attempting to fuse Chinese aesthetics with design styles of the West, young designers are creating a radical new identity for Chinese architecture by connecting new technologies and materials to traditional local craft and urban fabric. This newly-found national consciousness is rooted in an increasing self-awareness of the young creatives, rather than in a political programme. The most important role of Arup in this context is to help inspire the new creative identity of Chinese architecture. The architect Xu Tiantian comments:

> Modern Chinese architecture has been developing profoundly recently. It's not as mature as in Western countries—we're still learning the technical side—but the initial ideas are originating from our own culture. By incorporating the old and the new we have great potential for creativity. In general I found what's happening in China now is probably the most creative in this nation's history.[29]

An almost exponential economic growth and urbanisation also brought new opportunities for young artists and designers, generating an exciting, thriving and enthusiastic creative sector. Chinese graphic design, fashion, industrial design, art, new media and architecture are bound to outgrow their foreign inspiration and models in the very near future.

As a city with a history of creative exchange, Beijing has been injected with fresh energy via the avant-garde art scene. It reflects trends in contemporary society and the global economy, as well as being a magnet for investment. Beijing's new 'creative class' represents an important stimulus for economic growth that might slowly turn the country away from the prevailing wisdom of it being the world's biggest source of production and manufacturing.

The Beijing-based curator Ou Ning notes that, after more than ten years of dramatic economic growth, the costs of such development are starting to appear. Pollution and the excessive exploitation of rural resources resulting from the over-development of land—plus the disparity between urban and rural regions—all intensify the country's social contradictions.

> As a result, China is adjusting its industrial structure, developing 'smokeless' industries such as culture, media, entertainment, and information technology. The low-end manufacturing industry that used to rely on cheap labour is also required to evolve into a creative industry. After the Olympic Games, the saturation of the real-estate market will make architects turn to public and cultural buildings.[30]

City districts such as the Dashanzi Art Area bring together local and international avant-garde artists, designers, writers and musicians.

But the knowledge-economy in China is still developing, as its cities emerge from the latest frenzy of a fast-forward economy. As the country evolves and rediscovers its identity, the development of an original language, rather than chasing quick profit through low cost workers and cheap imitation, becomes increasingly important. Historian Martijn de Waal observes:

> Right now, creatives and managers are designing new technologies and building brands in the US. They hire coordinators in Hong Kong and outsource production in China. Could it be possible for Beijing to reverse this process? To become not only a target for production and consumption of ideas and technologies designed elsewhere? To become a true global metropolis and attract its own creative industry? To truly become a centre of creative design? In order to do so, the city needs to attract the new creative class. In the middle of all these new axes and zones of development, a demand will rise for places that will give them an identity, that will function both as places of inspiration and as a refuge, and that are a combination of underground breeding grounds and of advanced consumer culture.[31]

The electronics and information technology industries have both transformed lifestyles, allowing mass-consumerism to spread as widely as the communication networks reach. An interesting phenomenon in this context is the old Beijing area of Zhongguancun and its metamorphosis into a dynamic, busy 'electronic city': besides developing and selling hardware and software, it also pioneers new business models for corporate and research institutions.

When anticipating the future development of Beijing, young Chinese architects and designers admit that competition with their Western colleagues has been motivating, allowing them to consider smaller, low-tech and low-cost projects, as well as to rethink transportation systems and landscaping. While investors and political leaders, with a focus on instant success, may have dictated the fast pace of urban development, a more open decision-making process is bound to emerge that includes the critical issues of design, building maintenance and sustainability.

Ole Scheeren of OMA, a principal architect of the headquarters of CCTV, observes:

> Part of the appeal of the CCTV project is that it does not resolve itself entirely; it remains a challenging, engaging entity. There may be a mysterious capacity to the question of how it actually works while somehow we can sense how it works—it is very complicated to decipher exact mechanisms of its structure. I am sure this is also part of the challenge that the project presents to the public in general. The project is quite 'Chinese' as it does not revert to a one-liner interpretation, but balances in an almost

contradictory space of impressions and aspects. That has also heated up the debate and gained a very enthusiastic support, or got challenged by declaring the building morally incorrect.

However, the conservative architects and engineers that are protective of their own professional position have counterbalanced this by enthusiastic support of the new possibilities that the project pronounces. We hope to mobilise those for the future of architecture, or Chinese architecture. We are at a point in time in which a lot of foreigners have now significantly contributed to the architectural landscape of China and have injected a number of dominant elements in that landscape; yet at the same time, a new generation of Chinese architects is emerging, starting to search for their own position and expression.[32]

With this in mind, Arup's work in Beijing can therefore be seen as a contribution to China's process towards forming a new identity.

1 Sudjic, Deyan, "Cities on the edge of chaos", *The Observer*, 9 March 2008.

2 McCorquodale, Duncan, and Catherine Li, Steven Burrows, "Project: Beijing Olympic Stadium", in *Arup Interview Transcript*, 14 February 2008.

3 di Pietro Averlino, Antonio, "Plan of Sforzinda", *Trattato di architettura Florence*, c. 1465.

4 More, Thomas, *Utopia*, London: Penguin Books, 1969.

5 *Rites of Zhou (Zhouli)*, Jia Gongyan, ed., (fl. 655); Coleridge, Samuel Taylor, "Kubla Khan, or a Vision in a Dream. A Fragment", 1797, first published in 1816.

6 McLuhan, Marshall, and Quentin Fiore, *War and Peace in the Global Village*, New York: Bantam, 1968.

7 The fourth CIAM Congress, "The Functional City", *The Athens Charter*, 1933, first published in 1943.

8 Blake, Peter, *No Place Like Utopia: Modern Architecture and the Company We Kept*, New York: WW Norton, 1993.

9 Venturi, Robert, *The Complexity and Contradiction in Architecture*, New York: The Museum of Modern Art, second edition, 2002.

10 Lu, Duanfang, "Third World Modernism. Utopia, Modernity, and the People's Commune in China", in *Journal of Architectural Education*, vol. 60/3, 2007, p. 41.

11 McGuirk, Justin, "Shenzhen", in *Icon*, Issue 57, March 2008, pp. 52–61.

12 Koolhaas, Rem, "Junkspace", in *Content*, New York: Taschen, 2004.

13 Li, Lilian M, and Alison J Dray-Novey, Haili Kong, *Beijing*, New York: Palgrave Macmillan, 2007, p. 11.

14 Obrist, Hans Ulrich, "Rem Koolhaas", *Interviews 1*, Milan: Charta, 2003.

15 Ardill, Ralph, "Speech by the Marketing & Strategic Planning Director", *Imagination*—London Innovation Conference, 2003.

16 Li, Lilian M, and Alison J Dray-Novey, Haili Kong, *Beijing*.

17 Li, Lilian M, and Alison J Dray-Novey, Haili Kong, *Beijing*, pp. 17–18.

18 Paul Andreu, quoted in Shu, Kewen, et al, "Tiananmen guangchang duandaishi" [History of Tiananmen Square by period], *Sanlian Weekly*, Beijing, 4 May 2001.

19 McCorquodale, Duncan, and Catherine Li, Craig Gibbons, "Project: CCTV", in *Arup Interview Transcript*, 13 February 2008.

20 McCorquodale, Duncan, and Catherine Li, Michael Kwok, "Project: Various", *Arup Interview Transcript*, 24 January 2008.

21 McCorquodale, Duncan, and Catherine Li, Craig Gibbons, "Project: CCTV", *Arup Interview Transcript*, 13 February 2008.

22 McCorquodale, Duncan, and Catherine Li, Steven Burrows, "Project: Beijing Olympic Stadium", *Arup Interview Transcript*, 14 February 2008.

23 Li, Lilian M, and Alison J Dray-Novey, Haili Kong, *Beijing*.

24 McCorquodale, Duncan, and Catherine Li, Rory McGowan, Chris Carroll, Vesna Petresin, "Project: CCTV", *Arup Interview Transcript*, 29 February 2008.

25 Baron Pierre de Coubertin, 1863–1937, French historian and educator, founder of the International Olympic Committee.

26 McCorquodale, Duncan, and Catherine Li, Michael Kwok, "Project: Various", *Arup Interview Transcript*, 24 January 2008.

27 Glancey, Jonathan, "Secrets of the Bird's Nest", *The Guardian*, 11 February 2008.

28 Koolhaas, Rem, "Beijing Manifesto", *Wired*, Issue 12.08, August 2004, http://www.wired.com/wired/archive/12.08/beijing.html

29 Allen, Daniel, "China chasing an urban utopia", *Asia Times Online*, 18 May 2007, www.atimes.com.

30 Ning, Ou, "Email from China/Contributing to Icon", *Icon*, Yu Hsiao Hwei trans., Issue 057, March 2008, p. 67.

31 de Waal, Martijn, "Beijing and Beyond", *Beijing 798: Reflections on Art, Architecture and Society in China*, Huang Rei, ed. 2004, http://www.martijndewaal.nl/?p=32.

32 McCorquodale, Duncan, and Ole Scheeren, "Project: CCTV", *Arup Interview Transcript*, 11 March 2008.

ARUP IN BEIJING

China's transformation in recent years has been profound. The country's economy is rapidly expanding, and its accession in the year 2000 to the World Trade Organisation signalled to the world China's intention to become a major global economic player. This perception was reinforced in July 2001 when it won the right to host the 2008 Olympic Games, and with these two events acting as a catalyst, the country has been taking rapid steps towards opening up both its economy and its society.

As China's political and cultural capital, Beijing has become a focal point for many of these changes and is booming. The symbolism of the choice of the Beijing government to commission major new iconic venues to host and support the 2008 Beijing Olympic Games—together with the rapid rate of development in the city's new central business district—is clear; Beijing is keen that it hosts the "best ever" Olympics, and desires to take a place among the world's leading international cities, rivalling the likes of London, New York, Paris and Tokyo.

One firm, above all others, is closely linked to the striking transformation taking place in Beijing today. That firm is Arup.

Given the rapid pace of development, it is easy to forget that Beijing—and China as a whole—was effectively closed to non-Chinese firms prior to the year 2000. This makes it all the more remarkable that Arup can point to a presence of over 30 years in Hong Kong and a track record of working in mainland China since 1984, when the West still referred to the Chinese capital as "Peking". Almost a quarter of Arup's approximately 10,000 staff work in China, and its influence on China's development is significant.

In Beijing in particular, Arup has played a major role in helping shape the capital city's modern landscape. This is evident not only in the work it undertakes in partnership with a range of local and international architects—including Herzog & de Meuron, Rem Koolhaas' OMA, Foster + Partners, RMJM and Terry Farrell and Partners—but in the work it has done planning the city's transport infrastructure, and designing the associated infrastructure necessary to support Beijing's Olympics. And through its work in the wider China in promoting sustainable and energy-efficient design, and on the development of eco-cities, Arup is helping shape a more sustainable future for China.

Andrew Chan set up the China practice and is the firm's Deputy Chairman. He credits much of the firm's success in the region to its broad skill base and strong international reputation: "We have been involved in a whole variety of projects. You could say it is a strategy, but it is also because the firm is widely spread in terms of its expertise."

The way the firm established itself in Beijing is a good example:

> The Beijing government decided that the new central business district should not be near the Forbidden City, but should instead be out near the city's third ring road. In the initial competitions for work, we delivered one of the associated projects —a residential scheme, Central Park. That was the project that started us in Beijing.
>
> Call it strategy, call it instinct, but I said to my colleagues, the projects in this business district are multi-million square metre, mixed-use and of the highest quality; we've got to build our presence there. That was the instruction and it worked—at one stage we were the engineers on 60 per cent of the projects in the district.

This combination of insight and instinct helped Arup consolidate its foothold in mainland China, where its capabilities, in particular areas such as structural and fire engineering, infrastructure and environmental design are especially valued. And the firm's collaborative approach has made it much easier to consolidate its position with local Chinese professionals.

This emphasis on local relationships has helped the firm to push boundaries within China's built environment. And with a focus on high quality design,

Arup has made effective use of its global knowledge and experience and is applying this to the Chinese market. This is apparent not only in its designs, but also in its influence developing the built environment by helping to write regulations and establish best practice. Arup's global outlook is balanced by the emphasis it has placed on organic growth in China, recruiting local designers, engineers, business consultants and planners to the firm and promoting local talent to work with the best talent from across Arup's global skills.

ARUP AND BEIJING IN 2008

Arup is closely involved in many of the iconic and monumental projects commissioned to support the Olympics—both in terms of sporting venues and in supporting infrastructure. Among others, Arup has been involved in all of the following projects:

The Beijing National Stadium, also known as the 'Birds Nest', sits in the Olympic Green and is the main venue for the 2008 Olympics hosting the opening and closing ceremonies, as well as athletic track and field events. The building's vast scale and dramatic form creates a new icon for China and the city of Beijing.

The National Aquatics Center, also known as the 'Water Cube', is one of the most exciting sporting venues for the Beijing Olympic Games. The building's structural design is based on the natural formation of soap bubbles which create a random, organic appearance.

The Fencing Hall/National Convention Center hosts the fencing and air pistol events for the Beijing Games. It also houses the International Broadcasting Center and acts as the Main Press Center for journalists during the Games. Afterwards, the building will fulfil its design as a world-class exhibition, convention and retail centre.

Beijing Capital International Airport's new Terminal 3 is the gateway for visitors to the 2008 Games and allows the airport to cater for up to 90 million passengers a year by 2012. The iconic Terminal 3 will be one of the world's more environmentally sustainable airport terminal buildings.

The new headquarters of China Central Television (CCTV) is an extraordinary feat of design, redefining the form of skyscrapers and challenging the notion that such buildings should be built ever-higher. Comprising two leaning towers bent at 90 degrees at the top and bottom, which meet to form a continuous 'tube', the tower combines administration for CCTV with news, broadcasting, studios and programme production.

China World Trade Center Phase 3 is the tallest building in Beijing, standing at 330 metres tall and 73 storeys. It includes office accommodation, a five star hotel at the top of the building, as well as retail and entertainment venues.

Beijing South Rail Station is a landmark transport building that is a starting point for high-speed rail services to the regions of Tianjin and Shanghai, linking with the regional and local transport systems in Beijing. It is one of the largest stations in China, designed for a passenger turnover of 104 million passengers a year by 2030.

Beijing Parkview Green is one of China's largest sustainable architecture projects and one of the first in Beijing that has been designed to be environmentally sustainable. The complex includes a retail area, office and a six star hotel.

Nokia China's new headquarters, also known as the Nokia Green Building, is the first new-build LEED Gold Certified commercial office building in China —a highly regarded environmental rating scheme.

THE ARUP STORY

Arup is no ordinary firm. Founded in the UK in 1946 as a firm of structural engineers, it is today a multi-disciplinary practice of designers, engineers, planners and business consultants with over 100 offices in 37 countries.

The project that arguably first brought Arup to the world's attention was the structural design of the iconic Sydney Opera House in Australia, working with the Danish architect, Jørn Utzon, in the 1960s and making his unique design buildable. The firm's reputation was further enhanced with its work on the engineering design of the complex facade of the Centre Pompidou in Paris in the 1970s. In short, the list of projects that Arup has been responsible for over the years reads like a roll-call of the world's most innovative and sustainable buildings, infrastructure, planning and design projects.

The firm's reputation for honourable dealings and its over-arching humanitarian approach is unusual in today's business environment, and can be directly traced to the approach of its founder, the Danish designer, engineer and philosopher, Sir Ove Arup. Ove started the practice in 1946 with an emphasis on bringing together like-minded individuals from a broad range of disciplines and encouraging them to look beyond the constraints of their own particular specialisms to work in a fully integrated and holistic way. It was an approach he called "total architecture"—today called "total design".

This unconventional approach to design also extended to Arup's ownership structure. As the firm grew in both size and reputation, the original partners in the firm recognised that the most effective way of safeguarding the firm's future would be to transfer its ownership from the partners to a series of independent trusts. This would ensure that the firm was owned in trust on behalf of staff. In effect, this guaranteed the company's independence, and with no external shareholders, the firm is able to shape its own direction with no outside pressure or influence.

A light show on the GreenPix Zero Energy Media Wall, the largest colour light emitting diode (LED) light wall in the world.

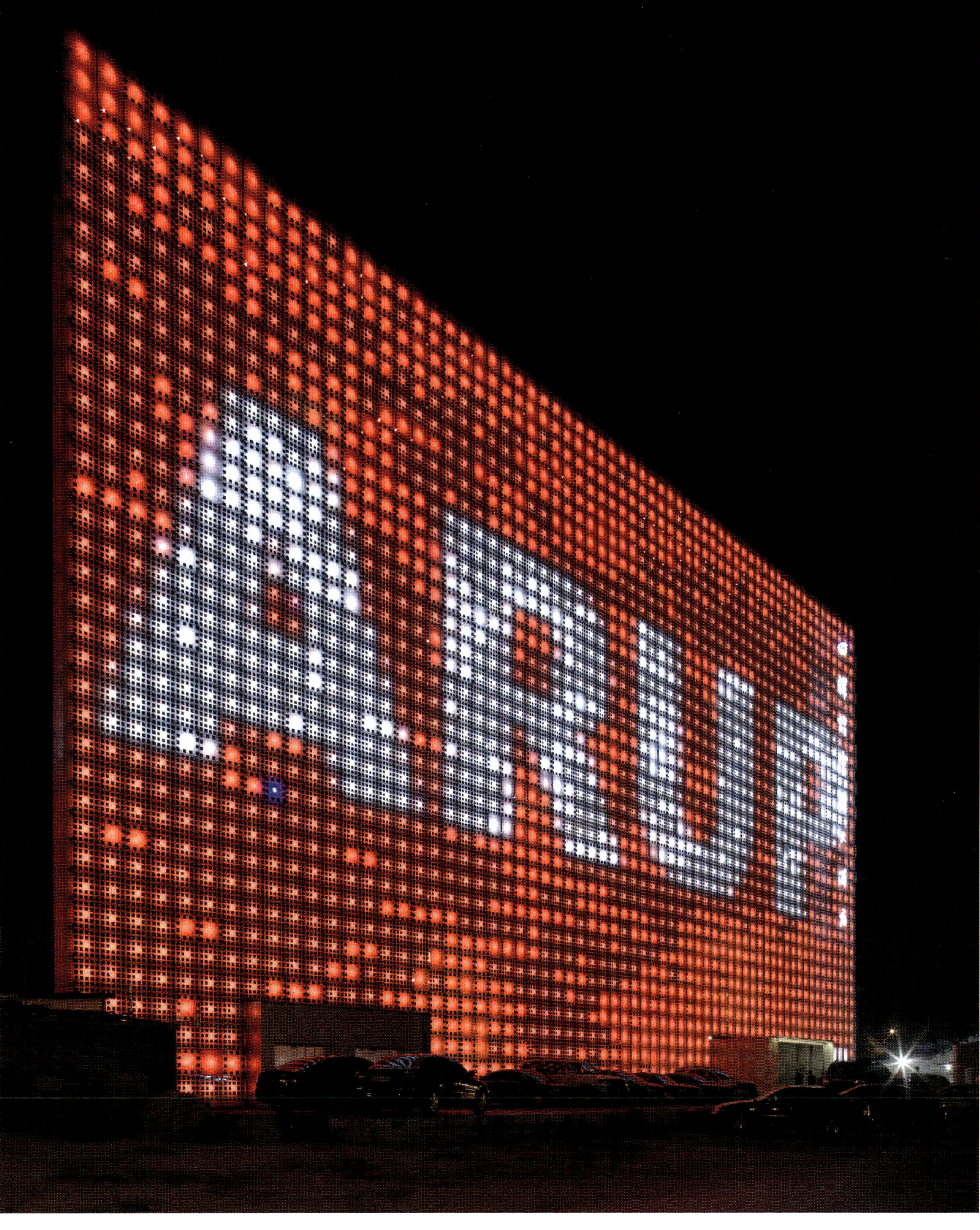

National Stadium

To best understand the legacy of the National Stadium, one has to understand the psyche of Beijing itself. Beijing wants its Olympics to be the most successful—ever. It wants buildings that are not just suitable to host the Olympics, but which also create a lasting legacy of iconic structures for the capital city, recognised far beyond China's borders. This internationalist ambition was seized upon by Herzog & de Meuron and Arup, whose inspiring design for the National Stadium quickly earned the nickname of the 'Bird's Nest'—thanks to the intricate nature of its structural design.

As the location for the track and field events and the opening and closing ceremonies for the 2008 Olympics, the National Stadium will be the Games' most ubiquitous structure. As befits this pivotal role, it has the largest seating capacity of any of Beijing's venues, with 91,000 seats—11,000 of which are temporary for the Games. It dominates the Olympic Green, which itself is the biggest that the modern Olympic movement has seen: ten times the size of the Athens Olympic Green and four times the size of that in Sydney.

The 'Bird's Nest' is also the most ambitious of all the Olympic venues and was the last to be completed. It was finished on schedule, with more than three months to spare before the start of the Games.

With the announcement in 2001 that China had won the right to host the Games, it quickly became apparent that the new National Stadium would be expected to be a visual showpiece, a strong design statement to champion the nation's modern ambitions. Architects from Arup's sports business had been working with Herzog & de Meuron on the Allianz Arena in Munich. The same team—architects from HDM, Arup and the Beijing Design Institute, CAG, together with engineers from Arup and CAG—began work in earnest on the design competition for the new stadium in March 2003.

(Previous pages) Photograph of the completed National Stadium. By day the muscular form glows with reflected sunlight; during the night the structure is illuminated against its dark surroundings.

(Opposite) Artist's impression of the National Stadium.

(Right) The 'Bird's Nest' on the opening day of the first test event, April 2008.

中咨监理
中信建设国华公司
朱景明青年突击队
李欢青年突击队
QUY50A

With more than 90,000 spectators to cater for, the most natural shape of the National Stadium is circular in order to give the maximum number of spectators the best view possible. Arup's first activities therefore focused on defining the shape and form of the circular stadium bowl—tasks which determined the seating pattern and placement of the concourses. The art of stadium design is in balancing many competing demands, including ensuring the seat placement is suitable for as wide a range of sporting activities as possible, and that there are good views for each and every spectator in the stadium. The design must allow the right amount of light and air circulation for the spectators and for the all-important track and pitch, and must also allow easy access to facilities, including lavatories and refreshments.

This sports architecture design directly informed the shape of the National Stadium's striking envelope. Athletics tracks are longer than they are wide, so the stadium form determined by Arup flows naturally and has a gracious curve.

The final Herzog & de Meuron and Arup proposal outlined a 70 metre high structure encased in twisted steel. The proposal had to pass the combined inspections of the voting public and a competition committee made up of six international architects as well as seven Chinese architects, structural designers, Olympic experts and officials. The 'Bird's Nest' emerged as a clear winner and, from the beginning, was well on its way to securing the hearts and minds of Beijing residents.

With a total floor area of 258,000 square metres, the 'Bird's Nest' is 330 metres long by 220 metres wide and has a height of just over 69 metres above pitch level. During the Games, it will provide a seating capacity of 91,000—to be reduced to 80,000 post-Olympics. The stadium seating design ensures that every spectator has uninterrupted sight-lines.

From the outside, the National Stadium's structural elements interweave in a seemingly-random grid—this design feature gives it the 'Bird's Nest' nickname, for its similarity to the appearance of interwoven twigs. But its initial design inspiration was from Chinese-styled 'crazed' pottery, typically found in Beijing markets.

The structure's vast scale and dramatic form together contribute to the lasting impression the National Stadium makes on the landscape. With the design purposefully provoking questions about which aspects are functional and which are aesthetic, it is this merging and blending of structure and facade that gives this stadium its iconic status.

(Previous pages) A construction shot of the 'Bird's Nest' showing part of the structure of the stadium.

(Opposite top) A construction shot showing roof details of the National Stadium.

(Opposite bottom) General view of the National Stadium, the shape and form of which was a critical factor in determining the seating pattern within the building.

In order to ensure a stadium that would be able to cope with Beijing's seismic activity, the structure comprises two parts: the concrete 'bowl' of the stadium; and the steel exterior facade and roof. It is this exterior shell, that reflects the 'bird's nest' metaphor, with spaces in the roof structure filled with ethylene tetra fluoro ethylene (ETFE) panels mounted on the inside. ETFE was also used by Arup in creating the translucent design of the National Aquatics Center, popularly known as the 'Water Cube'.

The muscular, concrete bowl of the National Stadium is designed to optimise spectator sight lines and minimise distance between the seats and the field where the action takes place. Arup was aware that, during athletic races, the most important view is of the running track finish line, but when used for football—one of the future uses of the stadium after the Olympics—the best views are of the centre line. So, in addition to the major challenge of getting everyone close enough in such a vast venue, it was critical that Arup's calculations on spectator views were precise because of the complexity of the large structure combined with trying to ensure more than 90,000 spectators all have a view.

The 'Bird's Nest' has met the functional and technical requirements of an Olympic stadium in a radical way. Its structure goes beyond conventional norms, presenting to the world a remarkable, aesthetically-pleasing piece of architecture and structural engineering. The twisted design of the shining steel will ensure that it will be a long time before another sports stadium matches the monumental form of Beijing's National Stadium.

(Opposite top) Night view of the masculine form of the 'Bird's Nest', with the feminine stucture of the National Aquatics Center, nicknamed the 'Water Cube', visible in the foreground.

(Opposite bottom) Details of the interior of the 'Bird's Nest' showing the unique design of the staircase.

(Following pages) The National Stadium showing the interaction of three elements–air, steel and stone.

National Aquatics Center

The 2008 Beijing Olympic Games is also a 'coming-out' party for China, celebrating its emergence as a major economic powerhouse on the world stage. It is also China's opportunity to show the rest of the world how it differs from conventional perceptions. The Beijing Organising Committee placed great importance on making the Games the most environmentally-friendly to date, thereby creating a legacy for sustainability to be at the heart of all future Olympic Games.

In setting the criteria for their approach to the 2008 Olympics, China identified three fundamental attributes: a 'people's' games, a 'high-tech' games and a 'green' games. The National Aquatics Center, popularly known as the 'Water Cube', is arguably the building that best embodies all three.

Designed to act as a giant greenhouse, the building appears to be built from a collection of oversized blue bubbles. These come together in the form of a blue, airy, cuboid that perfectly complements the red, muscular form of the National Stadium, located directly opposite the 'Water Cube' on Beijing's Olympic Green.

(Previous pages) At night the ETFE pillows are lit up using efficient light emitting diodes. Each pillow is individually programmable and can be made into any one of 16 million colours allowing a full light show using the facade alone.

(Opposite) The naturally-lit cafe in the northwest corner, showing the sculptural qualities of the internal spaces generated by the three-dimensional bubble structure.

(Right) The nature of the 'Water Cube' facade changes, reflecting different light and weather conditions. Here, a view of the building in lustrous sunlight.

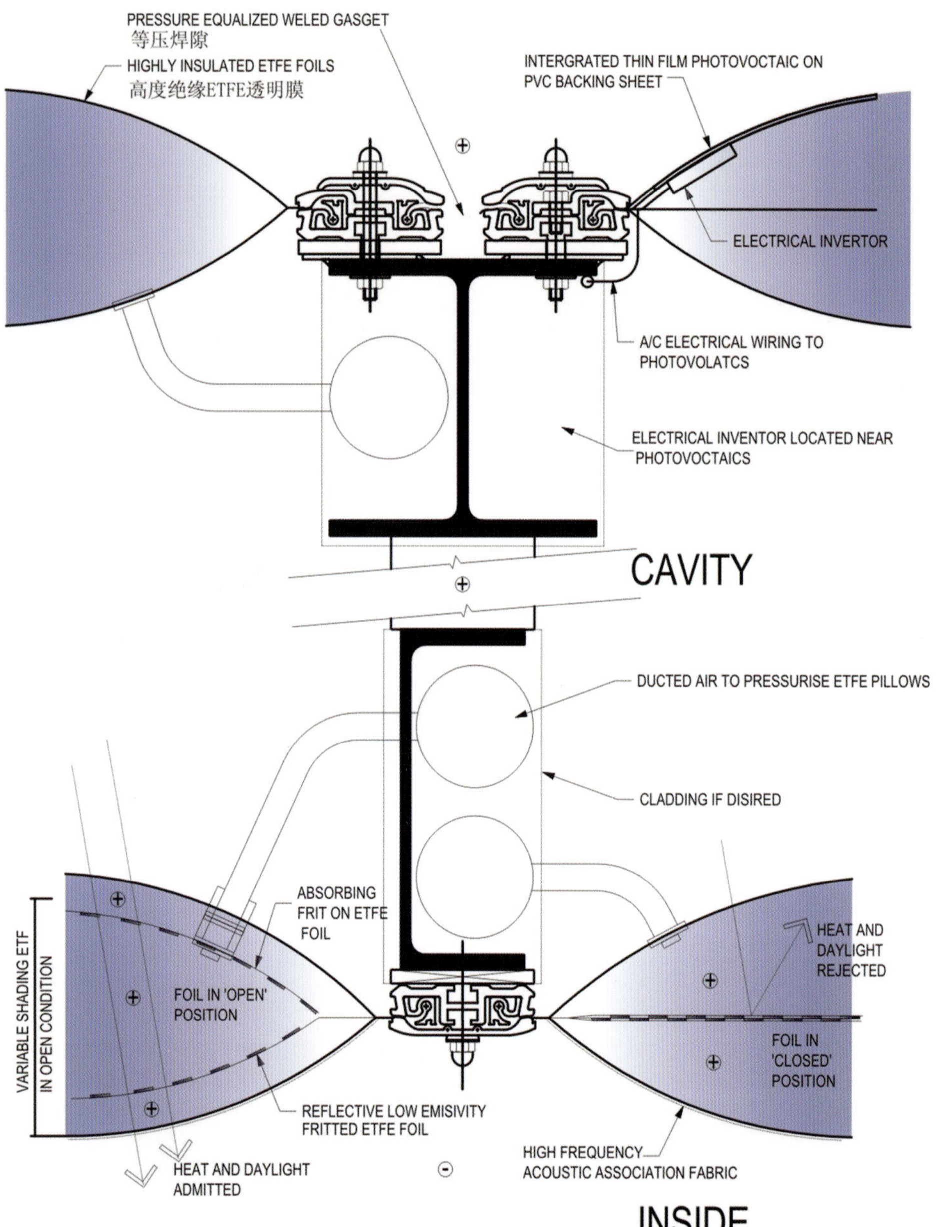

(Left) The roof and walls comprise two layers of ethylene tetra fluoro ethylene (ETFE) pillows. ETFE is a very inert, UV resistant, non-stick, transparent plastic. Inflated into pillow form, it spans up to 7.5 metres to form a very lightweight, resource efficient alternative to glazing. The pillows leak air vary slightly and are connected to air pipes and pumps to maintain inflation pressures.

(Opposite) The ETFE pillows have a silver dot pattern applied to the plastic film. Each pillow has its own density of silver dots that allows the optimal transfer of heat and light into the space behind. When the facade is in direct sunlight you see only the silver dots that turn the pillows into these bulbous metallic bubbles.

(Above and opposite) The steel structure of the walls is based on the geometry of a theoretically perfect array of soap bubbles. Therefore the pattern of the pillows is directly connected to the geometry of the structure to give an entirely three-dimensional experience.

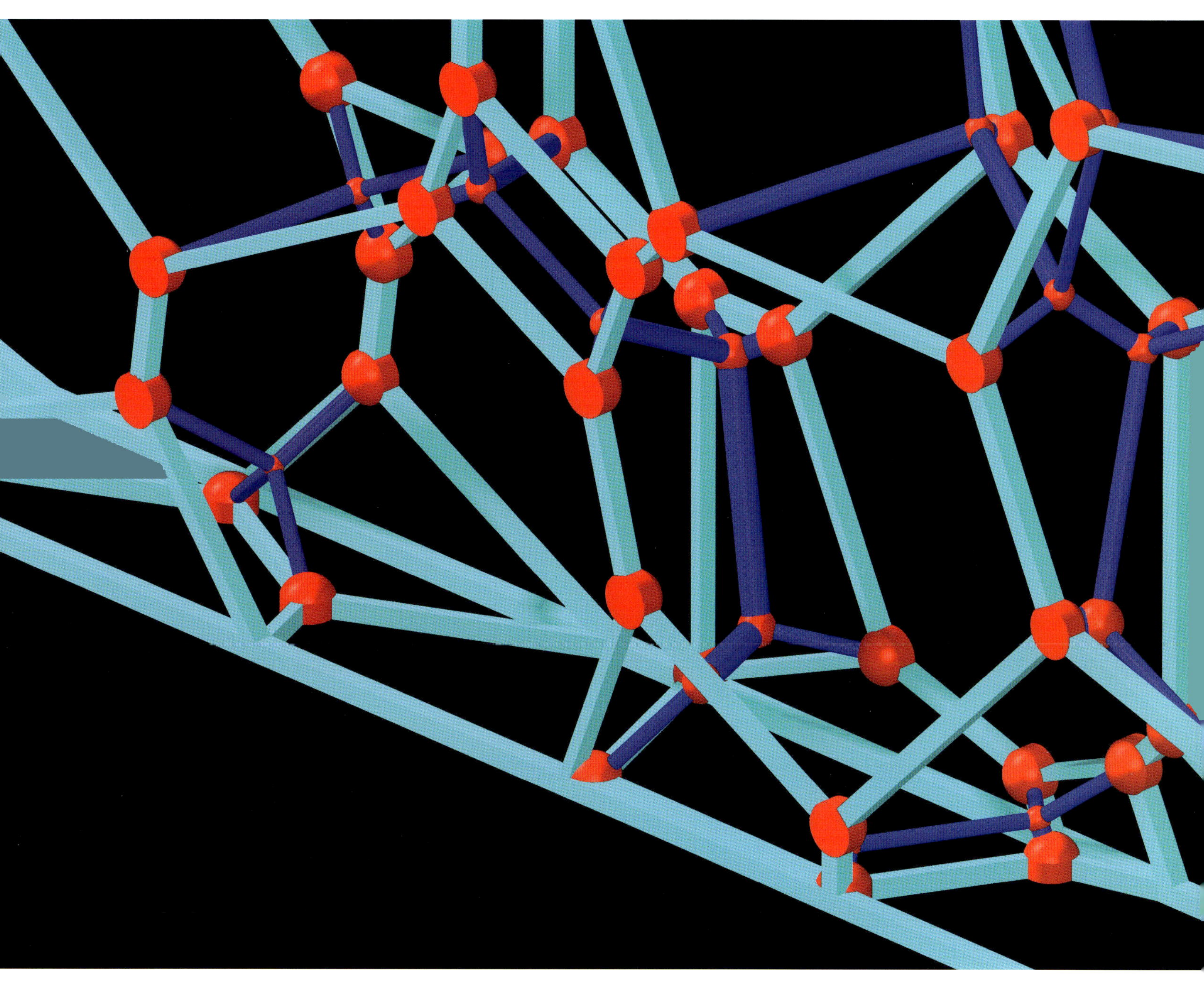

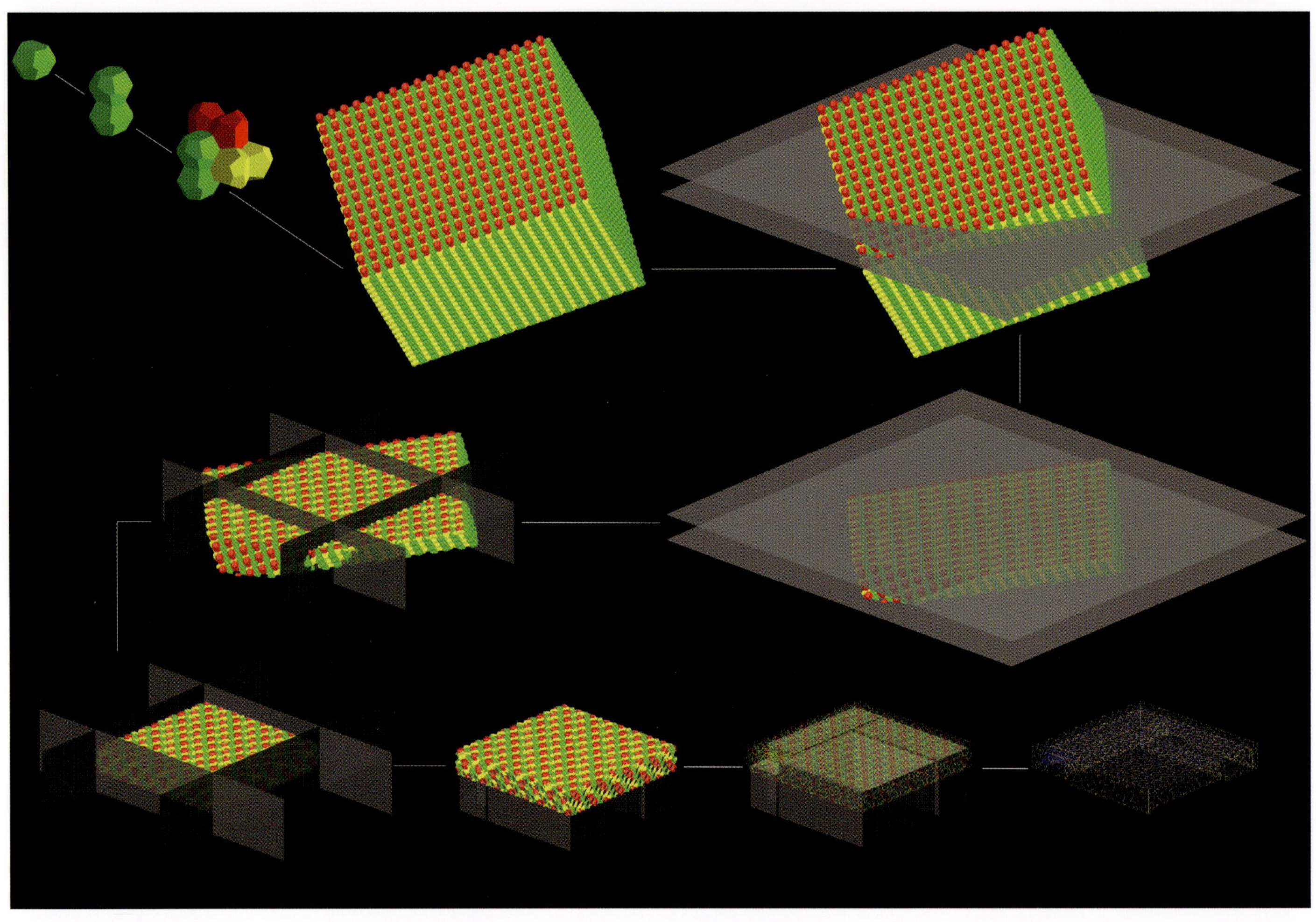

The 197 x 197 x 35 metre tall building was digitally 'carved' from a solid block of Weaire-Phelan Foam. The geometry of this foam is the optimal way of sub-dividing three-dimensional space and is also that of a perfect array of soap bubbles.

The roof and wall structures are perfectly continuous as they have been carved from the same block of Weaire-Phelan Foam. The resulting structure is lightweight, highly efficient and excellent at resisting earthquake loads.

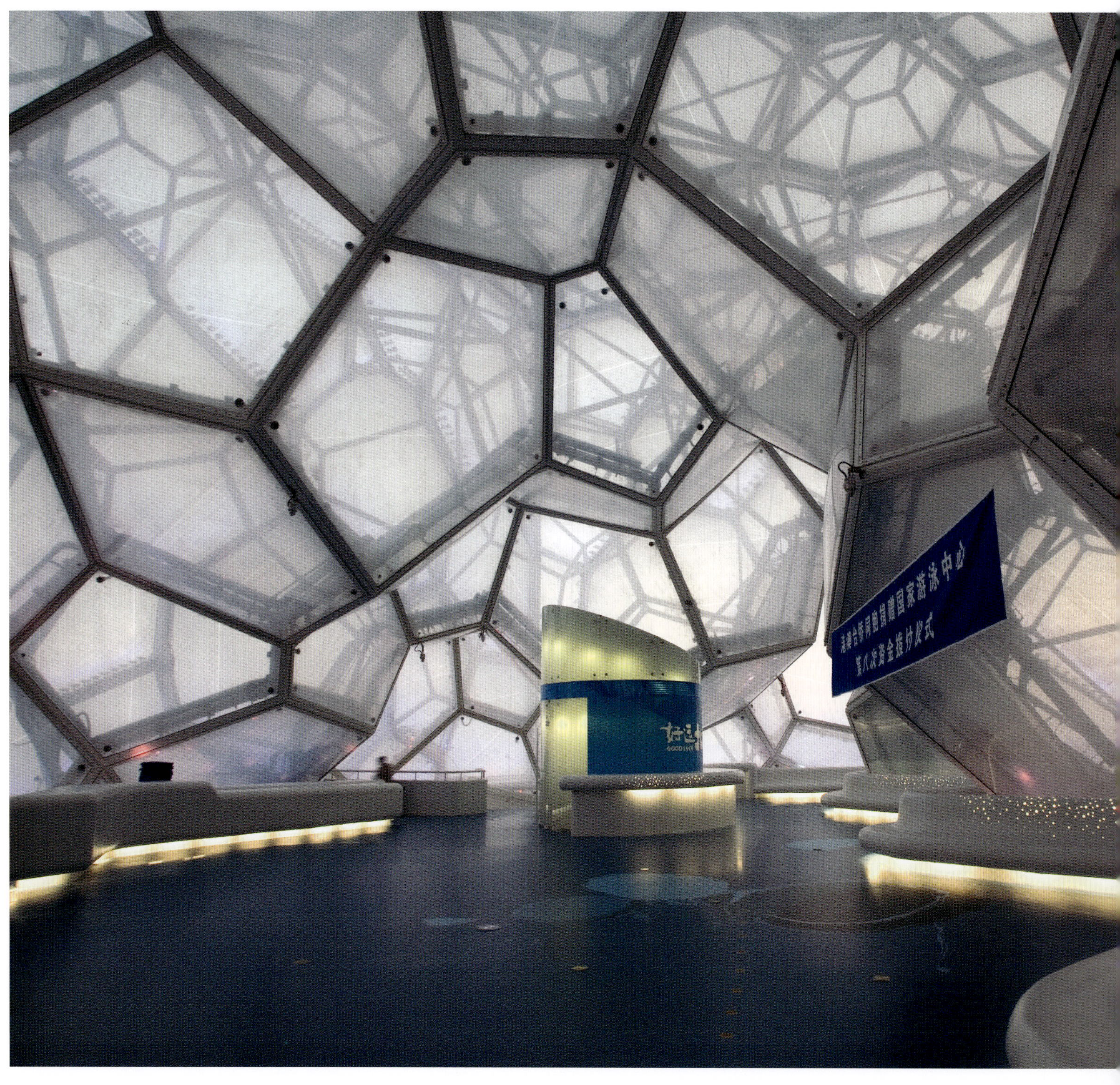
港澳台侨同胞捐赠国家游泳中心
第八次资金拨付仪式
GOOD LUCK

The 'Water Cube''s organic structure, which can be seen through the semi-transparent skin of the facade, is based upon the way soap bubbles join together to fill space. What is more, the translucence of the 'Water Cube''s revolutionary facade means that high levels of natural daylight flood into the blue-clad building, harnessing the sun's energy to heat both the building and pool water.

Arup has calculated that this greenhouse effect will reduce the energy consumption of the leisure pool hall by at least 30 per cent. The recyclable bubble cladding is key to the 'Water Cube''s aesthetic and sustainability aspirations. ETFE (ethylene tetra fluoro ethylene) was favoured by the design consortium of Arup, PTW and CCDI due to its inherent strength, but also because of its positive effect on the acoustics of the venue: sound passes through the material, rather than being reflected.

ETFE is also a better insulator than glass when shaped like inflated pillows. This also has the benefit of reinforcing the 'Water Cube''s inherent design. It seems an almost extraordinary coincidence that, when shaped in a way that echoes the bubble-vision of the consortium, that ETFE is also a better insulator. But this synergy is at the heart of the 'Water Cube'. With each facet having multiple uses and benefits, there are natural scales of economy with the materials used adding to the sustainability, and natural simplicity, of the structure.

Not just a better insulator than glass when shaped this way, ETFE is also far lighter. It weighs just one per cent of an equivalent glass panel, making the entire structure of the 'Water Cube' incredibly light—just 100 kilograms per square metre. This combination of strength and flexibility was important to Arup, acutely aware of the responsibilities of designing and engineering a building in a seismic zone.

Above the main entrance is the 'bubble bar', an area that has been subtracted from pure foam to allow the public to understand the original geometry of the perfect array of soap bubbles before the walls and roof were carved from it.

To finalise the 'Water Cube''s unique structure, Arup created a new computer technique to establish the size of all the individual elements of the building: too flimsy and it would lack the necessary robustness, too heavy and it would be in danger of collapse. Arup's computer techniques showed the extent to which every element in the 'Water Cube''s structure could bend and absorb energy. The bubble-like structure allows flexibility at an amazing 44,000 different points. Such thorough testing also alleviated concern about how the roof would cope with the very low temperatures of Beijing's winters and the weight of heavy snow storms. Testing revealed that the ETFE roof could withstand 17 times the weight of a normal Beijing snow load.

Arup found inspiration for the structure from the work of two Irish physics professors at Trinity College, Dublin, who had posed themselves the question: "What shape would perfect soap bubbles be when in a continuous array?" The answer was that the bubbles would arrange themselves in an order following a common natural pattern. Arup realised that a structure based on this unique geometry would be highly repetitive and therefore very buildable, while aesthetically appearing random and giving the facade a unique style. The result is a simple and stunning regular building shape that uses complex geometry to create a beautiful, organic feel.

The appearance of the 'Water Cube' forms a striking visual contrast to the neighbouring National Stadium. The 'Water Cube''s rectangular, blue structure is a feminine colour and shape that references the Chinese symbol of Earth. The National Stadium—also co-designed and engineered by Arup—is circular and painted a bold, masculine red. Its shape is symbolic of Heaven. Together, they create a symbolic duality between the elements.

Traditionally, Arup is renowned for supporting architecture through its engineering design work. However, the National Aquatics Center is an example of a genuine design partnership between Arup, PTW and CCDI, leading to a building that the combined design team calls their "common child". Their common child is a stunning and unique structure for Beijing, and the world.

(Opposite) The blue (female) 'Water Cube', based on a square that represents the earth, 'talks' to the red (male) 'Bird's Nest', based on a circle that represents the heavens.

(Following pages) The 'Water Cube' has been designed to complement the National Stadium. The buildings sit either side of the main north–south axis of Beijing that originates at the Forbidden City, seven kilometres to the south.

CATIC
CATIC

MEN'S 200M FREE
HEAT 5
1 LIM JAE YUB KOR
2 PEREIRA FABIO POR
3 PINI RYAN PNG
4 ZHANG LIN CHN
5 VIKSTROM C. SWE
6 KUBUSCH C. GER
7 HUANG SHAOHUA CHN
8 YEH JUAN MEX

Inside the main competition pool hall the levels of natural light are controlled to allow television broadcasting to have greater control using artificial lighting. When not being televised, the natural light is more than sufficient to illuminate the space.

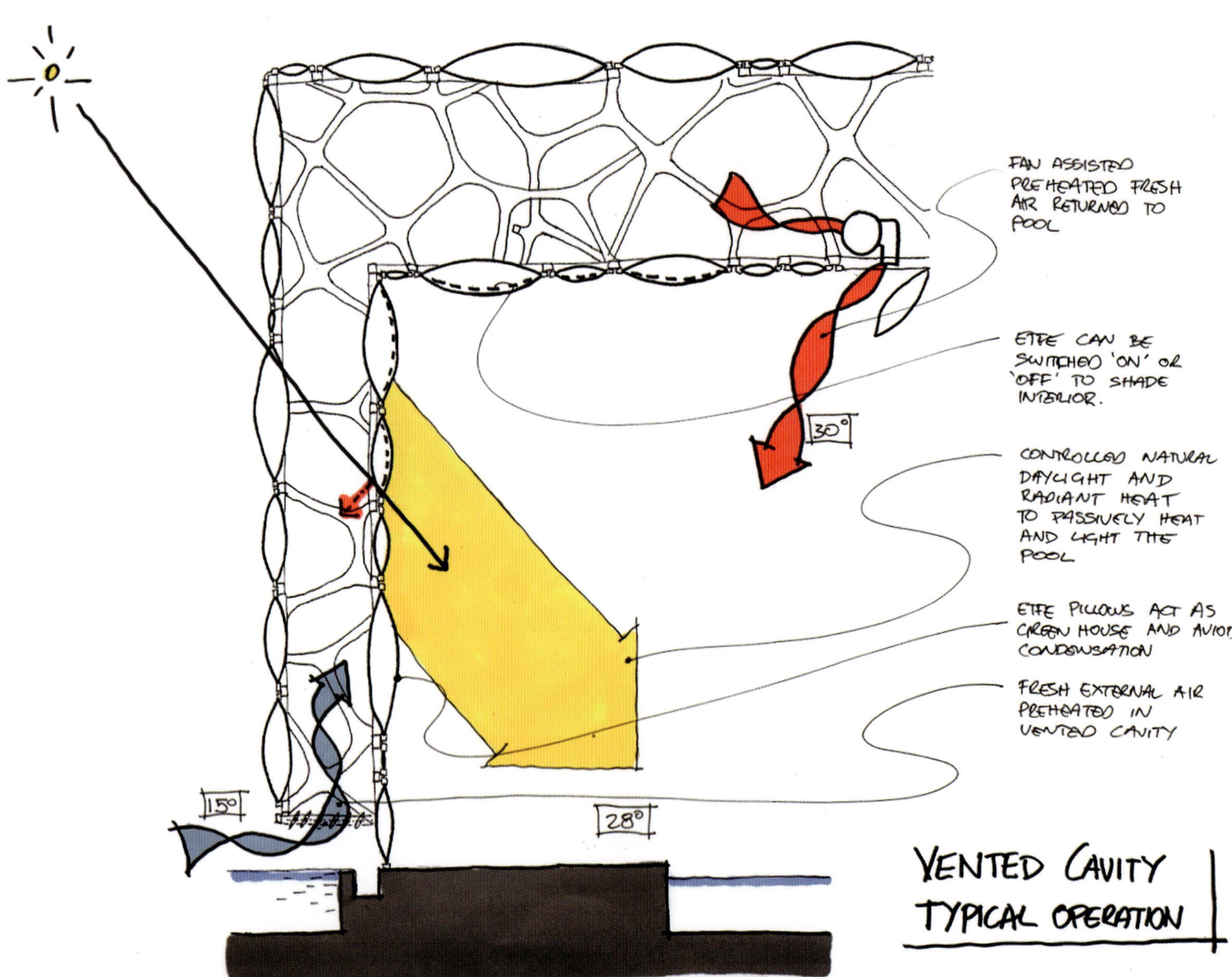
FAN ASSISTED PREHEATED FRESH AIR RETURNED TO POOL
ETFE CAN BE SWITCHED 'ON' OR 'OFF' TO SHADE INTERIOR.
CONTROLLED NATURAL DAYLIGHT AND RADIANT HEAT TO PASSIVELY HEAT AND LIGHT THE POOL
ETFE PILLOWS ACT AS GREEN HOUSE AND AVIOD CONDENSATION
FRESH EXTERNAL AIR PREHEATED IN VENTED CAVITY
30°
15°
28°
VENTED CAVITY TYPICAL OPERATION

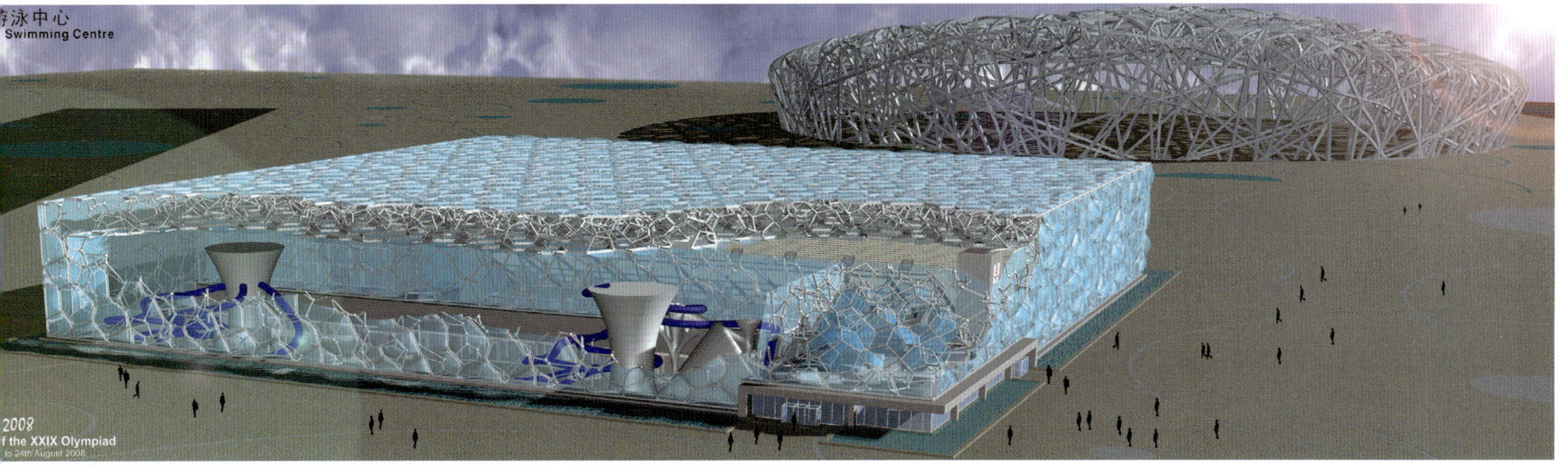

(Opposite) The 'Water Cube' has been designed as an insulated greenhouse. It collects 20 per cent of the solar energy falling on the building and uses it to heat the swimming pools. This saves 30 per cent of the energy required and is equivalent to covering the entire building with solar panels.

(Above) The entire structure was fully designed using a sequence of digital processes resulting in a comprehensive three-dimensional model that actually formed the construction documents.

Beijing Parkview Green

Beijing Parkview Green marks the beginning of a new approach to architecture in China. By putting energy efficiency at the centre of its commissioning process, the city is tackling air pollution head-on, setting the standard for a completely new approach in the region.

Arup worked with Integrated Design Associates on this mixed-use hotel, shopping and commercial hub, creating one of China's biggest sustainable architecture projects.

Not only is the structure the first in Beijing designed expressly with sustainability in mind, it is also the first to make use of a 'microclimate' as a means of minimising energy consumption throughout a building's lifetime.

Essentially an environmental shield, Beijing Parkview Green encases two nine-storey and two 18-storey buildings in a transparent 'envelope' made of glass and ethylene tetra fluoro ethylene (ETFE), the same material used in the National Aquatics Center ('Water Cube') and the National Stadium ('Bird's Nest'). The result is a microclimate: a contained environment, within which the effects of climate are both relatively uniform and easily modified. The ETFE shield creates a 'buffer zone' between each of the four buildings and their envelope, keeping the temperature constant. The buffer zone increases the thermal insulation in winter, reducing heat loss and saving energy.

(Opposite) Beijing Parkview Green under construction, Spring 2008.

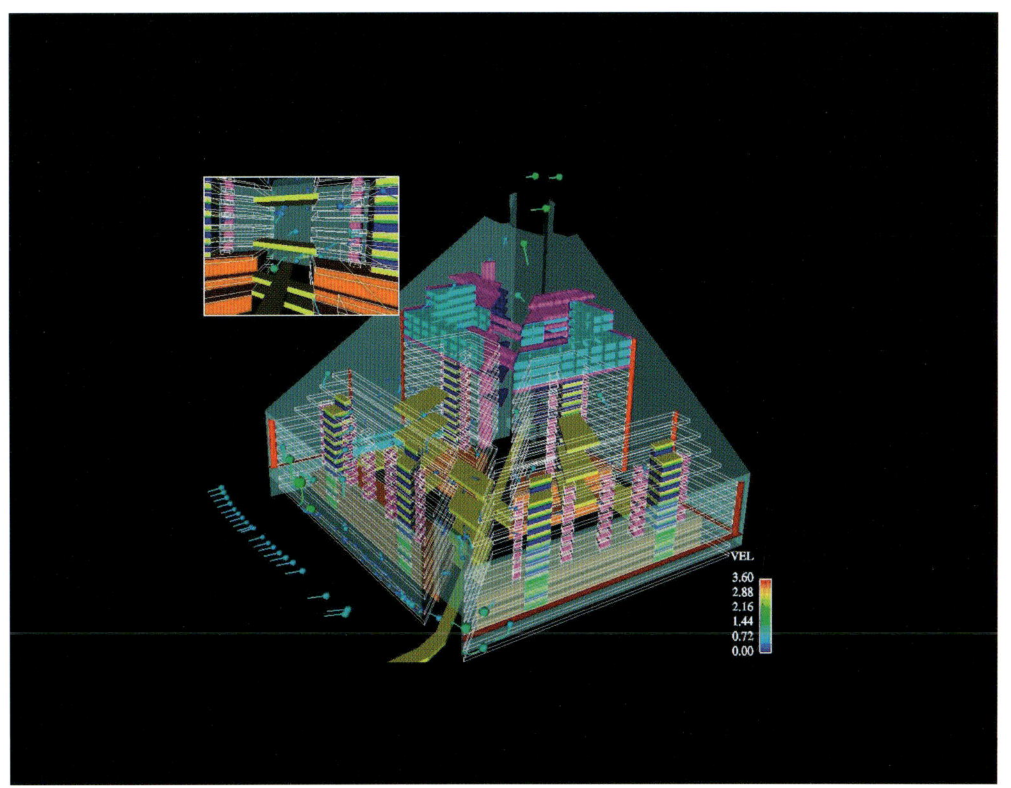

(Right) Computational Fluid Dynamics (CFD) analysis was used to verify the ventilation performance inside Beijing Parkview Green's microclimatic envelope. The envelope creates solar chimneys which provoke the movement of fresh air and bring natural ventilation into the interior space. Thermal currents and wind-driven ventilation enhance the upward air movement.

During hot summers, the envelope acts as a protective shield to prevent excessive solar heat gain being transmitted to the buildings. In winter, the microclimatic envelope behaves as an insulator, using controlled internal airflow to block the windy and freezing conditions outside.

The microclimatic envelope makes use of this hybrid ventilation during most of the year, even in the sand storm season. Temperature and air movement inside the envelope is relatively steady and moderate. This allows natural ventilation to be used inside the office blocks for almost the entire spring and autumn seasons, as well as during some of the cold winter months. The envelope is also designed as a windshield to protect the internal space and buildings from sand storms.

(Opposite) Ongoing construction allows a clear view of the towers that will sit within Parkview's microclimatic 'envelope'.

(Below) Artist's impression of the architectural design of Beijing Parkview Green.

The microclimate needs to be supplemented in summertime with a mechanism to let trapped heat escape. The Arup team devised ventilation louvres, to be installed at the top of the envelope. These act as chimneys, which allow the warmest air to escape, creating an upward air flow. As the air escapes, cooler air is drawn in from the bottom of the building, creating air movement and natural ventilation. The natural ventilation is supplemented by conventional air conditioning in summer and autumn, but at relatively low levels, making this an extremely energy-efficient structure.

While Beijing Parkview Green has been lauded for its innovative use of a microclimate, it is likely to be most significant long-term for its contribution to the development of sustainable building design in one of the world's fastest developing countries.

(Previous pages) External view of the Fencing Hall/National Convention Center just before the venue was completed.

(Above) Artist's impression of the auditorium inside the Fencing Hall/ National Convention Center.

(Right) Artist's impressions of the interior of the Fencing Hall/National Convention Center.

Fencing Hall/National Convention Center

With its curved roof that pays homage to traditional Chinese architecture, the Fencing Hall/National Convention Center is a striking addition to Beijing's Olympic Green and a major addition to the capital city's modern architecture. Together with the National Aquatics Center ('Water Cube') and the National Stadium ('Bird's Nest'), Arup's involvement in the Fencing Hall/Convention Center reinforces its influence on helping to shape the Beijing Olympic Green—the focal point for the Games where up to half of the Olympic events take place.

As the host venue for the main fencing and modern pentathlon events and its dual role as location of the International Broadcasting Center and the main Press Center for the Olympics, the Convention Center was always guaranteed to play a prominent role in the summer Games. In addition to its significant role as part of the city's sporting infrastructure, the Convention Center's long-term function is as a commercial development that addresses Beijing's need for international-standard exhibition, convention, banqueting and retail facilities.

At 400 metres in length and with a total floor area of 270,000 square metres, the innate flexibility of the space inside makes it ideal for hosting both the sporting events and the world's assembled media. The Convention Center is made up of a number of different buildings linked by large internal promenades. With a plenary hall, exhibition space, convention hall, office and retail space—all joined together by the 'street' zone, which stretches the length of the building—the Convention Center is characterised internally by long-span spaces which make the development extremely flexible in use.

For its Olympic use, the large spaces used for the fencing are complemented by a training hall on the Center's first floor which has a capacity for 1,800 spectators and holds 14 fencing strips; a warm-up hall on the Center's north side which features 12 fencing strips; and a television broadcast room on the south side of the Center's third floor. The modern pentathlon events will take place on the fourth floor of the Center's south side in a 7,000 square metres five-strip competition hall, holding up to 6,000 spectators.

As with many other of the Olympic venues, the Convention Center satisfies the requirement for the 2008 Games to be 'green', 'high-tech' and a 'people's' games. Landscaping features play a prominent role, with ornamental gardens providing a retreat for users of the facilities. The greenery of the interior is linked with that of the exterior through an elevated landscaped deck that will form a 'green oasis' within the Olympic park area. The development also consumes considerably less energy than other similarly-sized convention halls, and showcases a number of water-saving features.

Traditional air conditioning methods are replaced by an innovative energy-saving system in which a subsided garden seven metres below ground level is used to provide air conditioning by current convection. It works on the principle that the temperature of air is lower in the garden than in the higher temperature indoor spaces in the Convention Center above. This difference results in a natural convection heat transfer mechanism in which hot air is cooled naturally—saving an estimated 380,000 kilowatts each year.

The design of the enormous 60,000 square metres roof provides the building with a distinct profile, both in elevation and in plan. It serves as a major architectural statement while providing continuous cover to the entire development. The full-height glass facade along the front face of the building reinforces the minimalist structure and the elegance of the architectural design.

A view showing the facade of the Fencing Hall/National Convention Center just prior to completion.

The curved roof of the Fencing Hall/National Convention Center pays homage to traditional Chinese architecture.

The roof is also a major environmental feature of the building. Its shape mirrors that of a traditional Chinese flying roof, with corners that curve upwards to create an inverted arch. This structural form acts as a giant rainwater collector—with a multi-layer roof structure to minimise the noise of rainfall. The collected water is then channelled into a water treatment facility, after which it is used in water landscaping around the Convention Center.

The Convention Center also contains many symbolic elements of traditional Chinese culture that have been incorporated into the design. As well as the upturned roof, the building location itself contains important messages of unification and communication—two important motifs in Chinese culture. Located on a site that symbolically links the Qin and the Han dynasties, the building's bridge metaphor reflects these two dynasties whose influence saw the creation of a unified multi-racial nation in China—the Period of Great Unification.

After the Games, the building's flexible design will see it converted into a multi-functional convention hall with vast exhibition spaces, and plenary rooms with a capacity of up to 6,000 people. It will also have a much-needed banqueting room that can accommodate up to 3,000 guests. With this legacy use assured, Beijing has an international-standard convention centre on its doorstep.

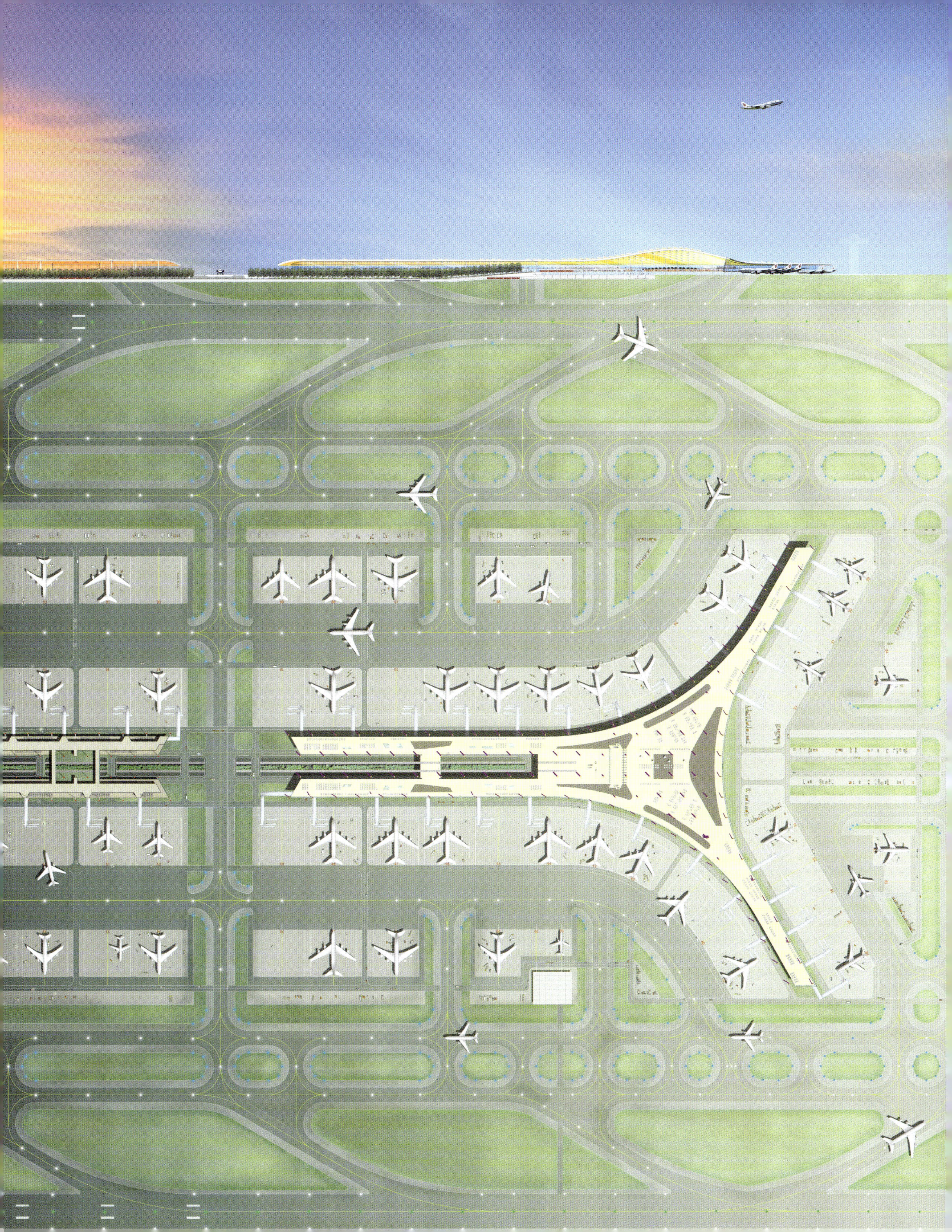

Beijing Capital International Airport Terminal 3

Beijing Capital International Airport Terminal 3 is a striking symbol of the rapid economic, technological and architectural growth taking place in China today. Having been conceived, constructed and commissioned in the space of just over four years, this iconic terminal is the first experience of China for the millions of visitors arriving in Beijing for the 2008 Olympic Games. With its eye-catching design, its vast-but-welcoming scale and its smooth and efficient passenger experience, the airport terminal speaks volumes about the image that China wants to project to the world.

This is arguably the world's most advanced terminal, and is both an architectural icon and a major technical achievement. Already China's busiest airport, the addition of Terminal 3 and a third runway will enable the airport to cater to more than 80 million passengers per year. It sets a global standard for positive passenger experience and energy efficiency in airport terminal design.

Beijing Capital International Airport Terminal 3 was designed by a team comprising Arup, Dutch airport planners, NACO, and architects Foster + Partners. The structure builds upon the design principles established by Arup and Foster + Partners for London's Stansted Airport, and the Chek Lap Kok Airport in Hong Kong.

(Previous pages) Plan and elevation of the new Beijing Capital International Airport Terminal 3.

(Opposite) Longitudinal view of the basement under construction.

(Right) Internal views of the newly completed terminal building, revealing the mixture of natural and red and gold lighting.

One of the fundamental principles governing the design was to make it as welcoming as possible. The terminal building is bathed in a mixture of natural light and a red and gold lighting scheme, while the physical shape of the terminal and its slatted red ceiling invites visitors to make their way through the building towards the major destination points. This subtle effect—of being guided by the direction of the roof and the arc of the building ahead—serves to dramatically reduce the amount of time it takes to navigate through the airport, making transfer times shorter, and cutting down the distances travelled between the terminal's areas.

Supporting this is the terminal's advanced baggage-handling system. 330 check-in desks connected to a total of 50 kilometres of high-speed tub conveyors controlled by sophisticated IT and automation systems make it one of the most advanced systems in the world.

With a floor area of 1.3 million square metres and measuring 800 metres at its widest point, the building's scale is immense. The functional base is wrapped in a roof that appears to float on tapering slender columns, while admitting an abundance of natural light. This structural concept also allows it to withstand Beijing's pronounced seismic activity. The roof columns have been individually tuned so as to be able to provide both strength and flexibility, ensuring that the roof can shift safely in the event of an earthquake.

(Opposite) Passenger circulation in the airport is enhanced by the buildings structural columns and directional lighting scheme.

(Right) A view of the airport's baggage-handling area.

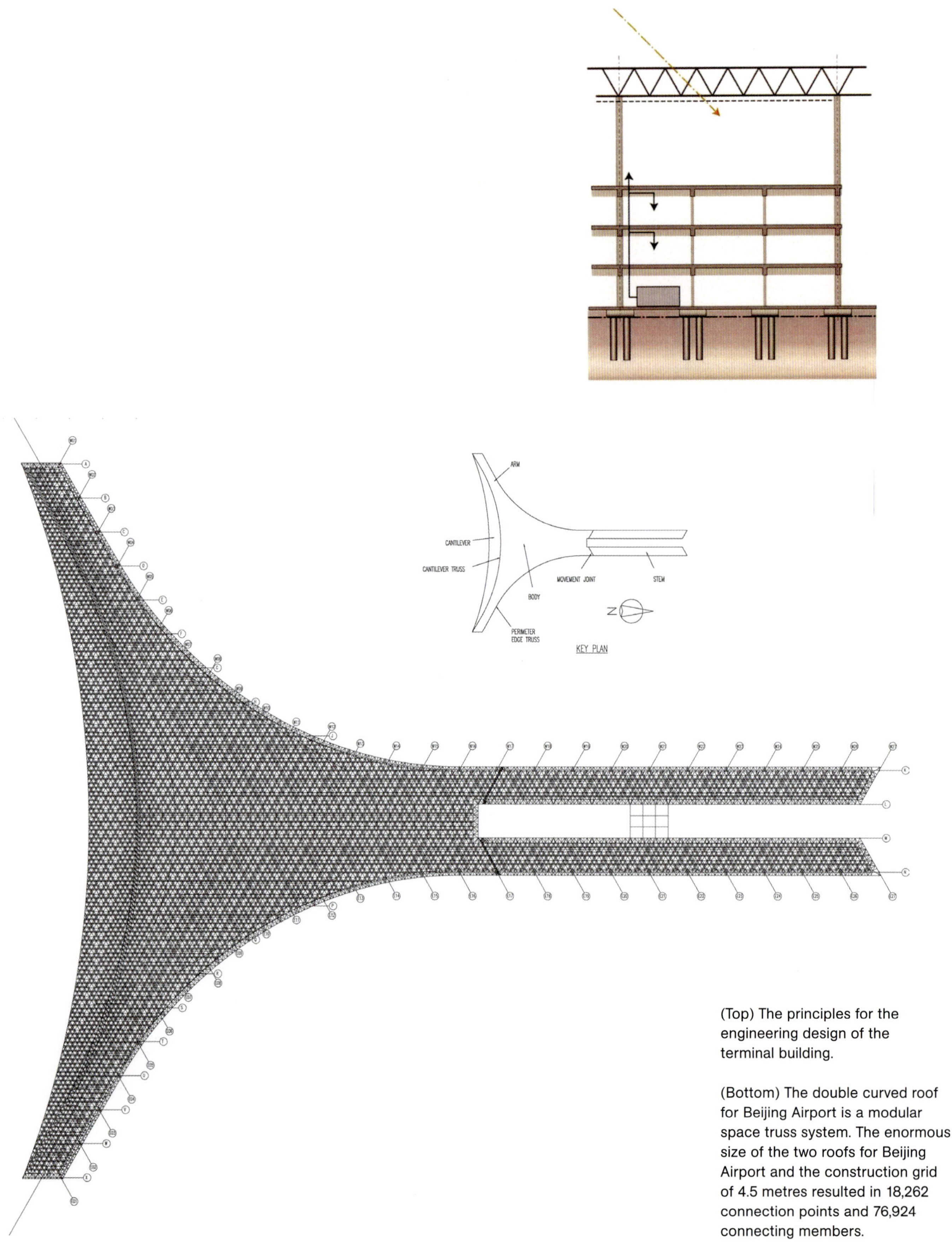

(Top) The principles for the engineering design of the terminal building.

(Bottom) The double curved roof for Beijing Airport is a modular space truss system. The enormous size of the two roofs for Beijing Airport and the construction grid of 4.5 metres resulted in 18,262 connection points and 76,924 connecting members.

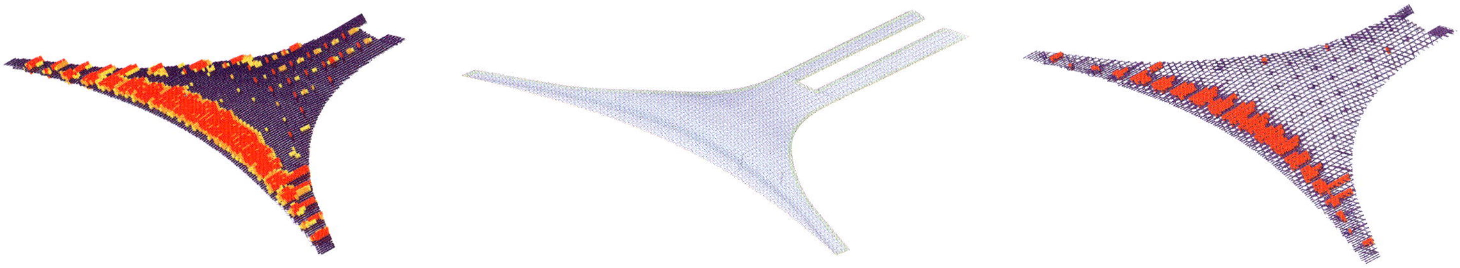

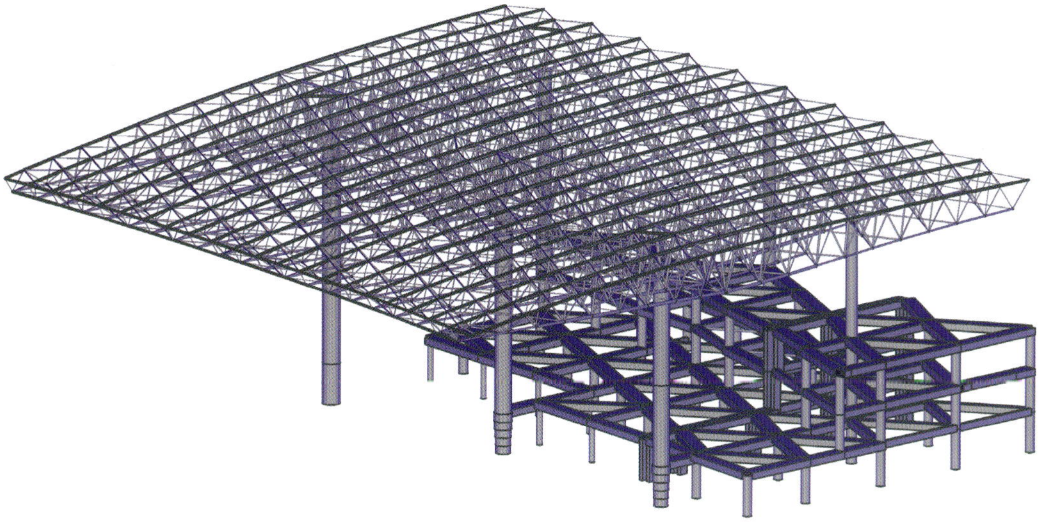

(Top and middle) In order to achieve an optimised steel weight it was essential that the members are sized individually rather than grouped and a certain steel profile pre allocated to the member. Maximum member utilisation, and therefore minimum steel weight, was achieved in an iterative process in which members size was gradually increased until a utilisation of 100 per cent, or slightly below, was achieved.

(Bottom) The structure of the building is a reinforced concrete frame up to five storeys high, above two levels of basement and beneath a steel roof. The steel roof is joint-free. Hollow steel columns, two metres in diameter, support the roof and cantilever up from the reinforced concrete base. Extensive geometric refinement was required to tune the relative stiffness of these columns and to ensure that the maximum sway under seismically-induced forces was kept within acceptable limits.

A strong visual and environmental feature of the terminal building is the use of roof lights, which are an integral part of the energy-efficient design of Beijing Capital International Airport Terminal 3. Angled southeast on the curving roof, these lights capture the thermal energy used to heat the building on winter mornings—thus helping to minimise the terminal's energy consumption. Their small size also helps reduce the building's cooling requirements during warm summer months.

The design also incorporates other passive environmental technologies, including a dual-water system that reduces overall usage. With energy consumption minimised through the incorporation of shading; natural heating and cooling used as often as possible; and the effective use of natural lighting, Beijing Capital International Airport Terminal 3 is one of the world's most energy-efficient airport terminal buildings.

Passengers leaving the terminal building find themselves standing under an awe-inspiring 800 metre cantilevered roof that protects the pick-up and drop-off points from the elements. A newly built station for high-speed rail connects the airport to Dongzhimen station in central Beijing in just under 15 minutes. Over 50 pick-up bays cater for up to 2,500 taxis at peak times, while over 30 bays are provided for buses. Undercover short-term parking is provided for over 7,000 cars.

Beijing Capital International Airport Terminal 3 is a project originally inspired by the 2008 Olympic Games, but which was delivered—with enormous skill and flair—to fulfill a real economic need at great speed. It has been a truly Olympian achievement for all involved in its conception.

(Bottom left) Daylight provides a sustainable alternative to electric lighting; however the effects of daylight can, at the same time, be both beneficial and detrimental. Direct solar radiation brings increased thermal problems along with glare, while sunlight can be invigorating and induce a sense of well-being. All of these are important to both the staff and passengers, particularly in enhancing their experience of the airport and in providing orientation.

(Bottom right) Study of sun penetration used in developing the passive shading geometry of the roof light.

(Opposite) Details of the roof light, showing the visual focus used in assisting orientation within the terminal building.

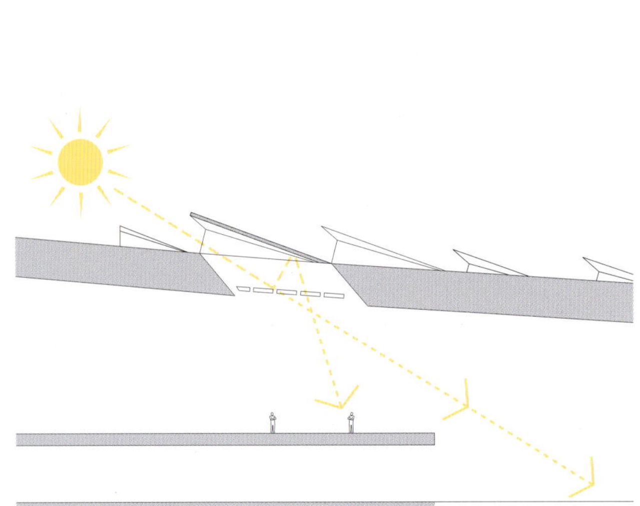

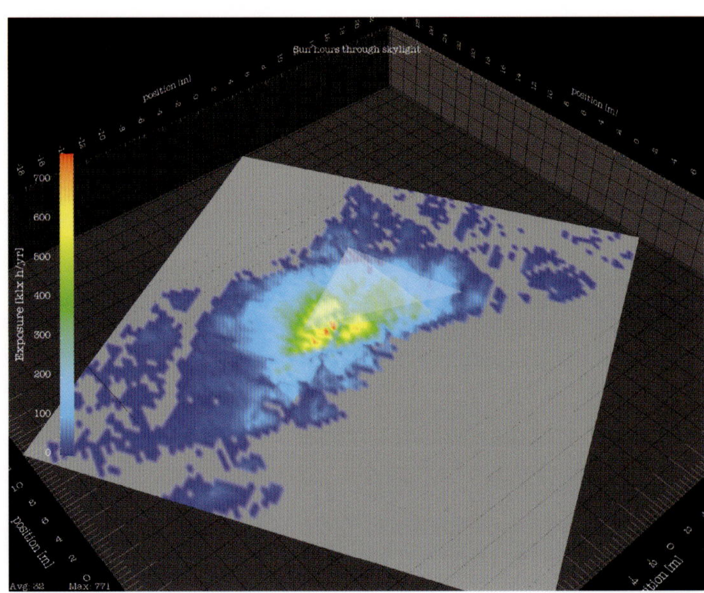

C

(Previous pages) The connecting railway station between the airport and Beijing at night. The roof of the station spans across all the tracks and platforms to ensure that there is the maximum clear access for passengers and trains. The steel arches span almost 130 metres and are supported by reinforced concrete buttresses, which pass down through the structure of the car park. The roof is fully glazed.

(Opposite) Photograph showing the cantilevered part of the roof of the terminal building.

(Right) Artist's impression of the new Terminal 3.

China Central Television's Headquarters

Listed by *Time* magazine as one of the ten new architectural wonders of the world, the new headquarters of China Central Television (CCTV) breaks many of the conventional wisdoms about skyscraper design. It is a direct challenge to the assumption that 'tall is best', and is a significant stake in the ground for Beijing's—and China's—desire to be taken seriously on the world stage. With such a monumental and iconic design, the world is sitting up and taking notice.

It is no coincidence that Arup is the thread that links this groundbreaking structure with those other uniquely-designed and engineered buildings in Beijing: the National Stadium ('Bird's Nest') and the National Aquatics Center ('Water Cube'). Each has presented unique design challenges and each has a claim to be considered among the world's most innovative and iconic designs.

The sheer audacity of CCTV's new headquarters has afforded it the widest attention of all the newly-conceived structures in Beijing. Only images can adequately explain the form of the structure, consisting as it does of two colossal towers that rise at awkward angles to a height greater than the landmark HSBC building in Hong Kong and equal to that of One Canada Square in London's financial district. Both towers are joined at the top by a bridge that juts out at a bizarre right angle.

(Previous pages) Artist's impression of the new Chinese Central Television (CCTV) headquarters.

(Opposite) View of China Central Television's headquarters under construction.

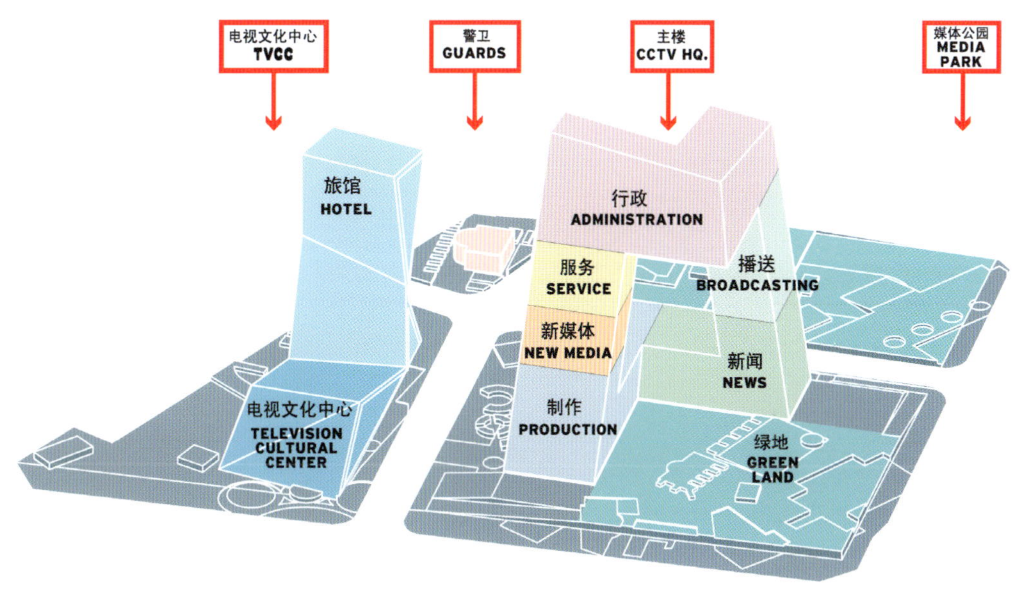

(Right) OMA decided that by housing all of the facility in one building, it should be possible to break down the 'ghettos' that tend to form in a complex and compartmentalised process like the making of TV programmes, creating a building whose layout in three dimensions would lead all those involved—the creative people, the producers, the technicians, the administrators—to mix and produce a better end-product more economically and efficiently. A second building, TVCC, contains a five star hotel as well as a 1,500 seat theatre, cinemas and studios.

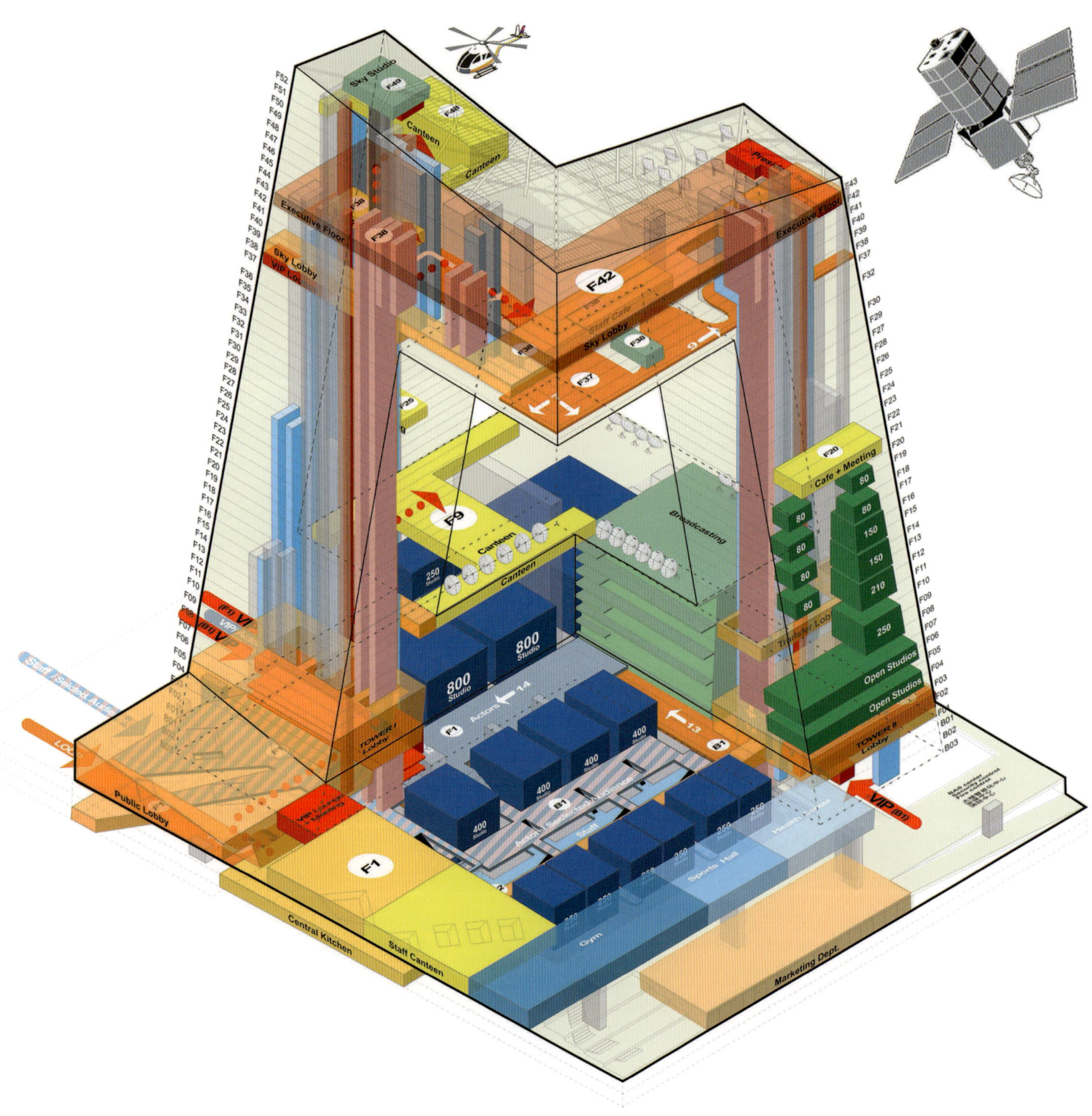
Sky Studio
Canteen
Executive Floor
Sky Lobby
F42
Staff Cafe
F37
F20
Cafe + Meeting
F9
Canteen
Broadcasting
Transfer Lobby
800 Studio
Actors
Open Studios
TOWER I Lobby
TOWER II Lobby
Public Lobby
F1
Central Kitchen
Staff Canteen
Gym
Sports Hall
Marketing Dept.
VIP (B1)

(Opposite) CCTV tower programme distribution. The winning design combined administration and offices, news and broadcasting, programme production and services, the entire TV production process, in a single loop of interconnected activities. Many of the larger spaces, including major studios, are located in the ten-storey podium section of the building. The building also contains public access, including a viewing gallery at the bottom floor of the overhang section.

(Right) Development and bracing pattern. The primary structure of the CCTV building engages the entire facade, creating in essence an external continuous tube system. Adopting this approach gave proportions that could resist the huge forces generated by the cranked and leaning form, as well as extreme seismic and wind events. This 'tube' is formed by fully bracing all sides of the facade. The continuous tube system is ideally suited to deal with the nature and intensity of the loading on the building: it is a versatile, efficient structure which can bridge between the towers, provide sufficient strength and stiffness to the building, and deliver loads to the foundations in the most favourable possible distribution, given the geometry. The complex shape of the building meant that the stresses were not uniform around the structure, but experienced a large amount of variation. Instead of changing the size of each brace to suit its individual force, the regular 'base' pattern was tuned or optimised by adding or removing diagonals to match the strength and stiffness requirements of the design. The result visually expresses the pattern of forces within the structure and is an important aesthetic aspect of the cladding system.

The architects OMA (Office of Metropolitan Architecture) and Arup have collaboratively made the impossible possible. The brief called for all of CCTV's functions for production, management and administration, to be contained on the selected site—albeit that this might not be possible in one building. In their architectural response OMA decided that integrating all the functions in one building would have the benefit of breaking down the silos that tend to form in an organisation. OMA and Arup devised a building whose layout in three dimensions would force all those in it to mix, integrate and interact. The aim is for traditional compartments to be broken down, with an end-product that is more economic, efficient and creative.

The design for the 473,000 square metre, 234 metre tall building combines the entire process of China Central Television's operations—administration and offices with news and broadcasting, programme production and services—in a single loop of interconnected activities around the four elements of the building: the nine-storey 'base'; the two leaning towers that slope at a precarious ten degree angle towards each other; and the nine- to 14-storey 'overhang' situated 36 storeys up in the building. To put it into context, the Leaning Tower of Pisa is a mere 3.97 degrees in incline.

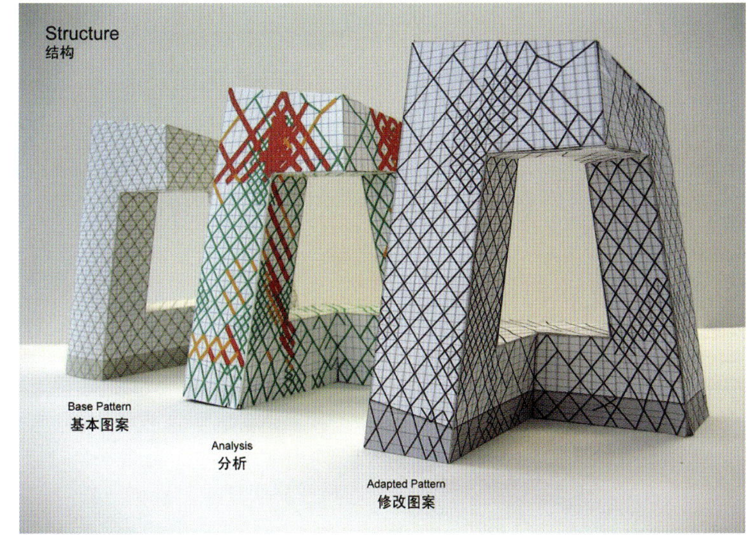

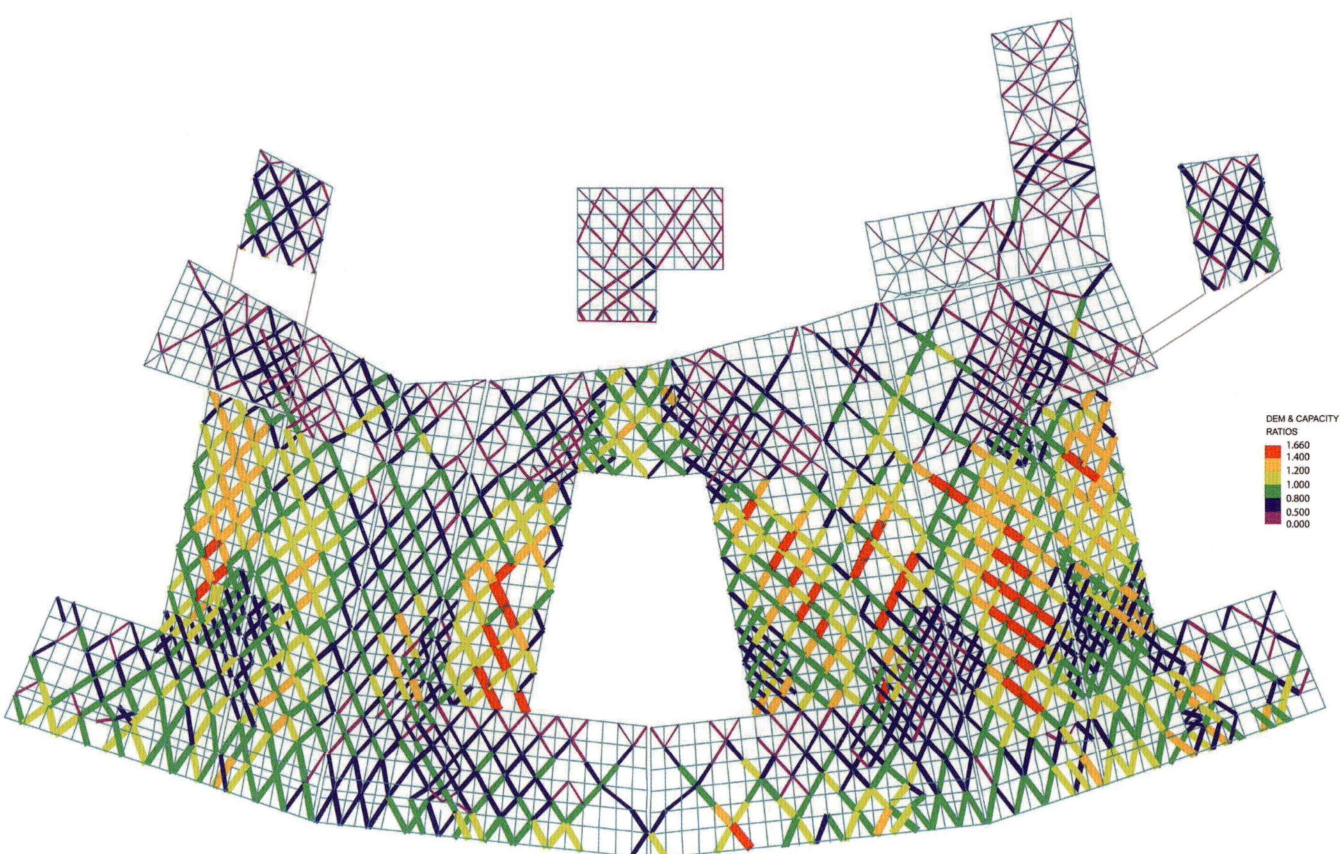

(Above) An unfolded stress pattern view of the structure was developed to clearly display the analysis results of all faces of the building in one view. This enabled the design team to visually process the results quickly, while keeping the architect up-to-date and involved in the development of the pattern.

(Opposite left) Joint finite element model analysis and installation. The forces from the braces and beams must be transfered through and into the column without causing overstress. The connection is formed by creating large 'butterfly' plates, which extend from the faces of the column and then connect with the braces and the edge beams.

(Opposite right) A detail of the 'butterfly' plates and connections to the braces and edge beams.

The gravity-defying structure of the headquarters of CCTV has redefined the traditional form of skyscrapers, and posed unparalled structural challenges for Arup's design engineers. Notably, prior to being connected, the two towers—in response to Beijing's environmental conditions—would move independently of each other. The strategy for joining these two towers at the top was heavily influenced by these structural implications.

A building as vast as CCTV's headquarters is subject to enormous loads and applied forces. The largest column of the building, for instance, supports a weight of 17,700 tonnes—roughly the equivalent of 44 fully-laden Jumbo jets. Most importantly, the building must be able to cope with the risk of earthquakes. As a result, a structural system of diagonal grids, or 'diagrids', was created, comprising leaning columns, triangulated bracings and horizontal beams. These diagrids are visible in the building's facade, representing the distribution of gravitational and lateral forces throughout the structure of the building. This system supports the building's weight while giving it the ability to withstand a high level of seismic activity.

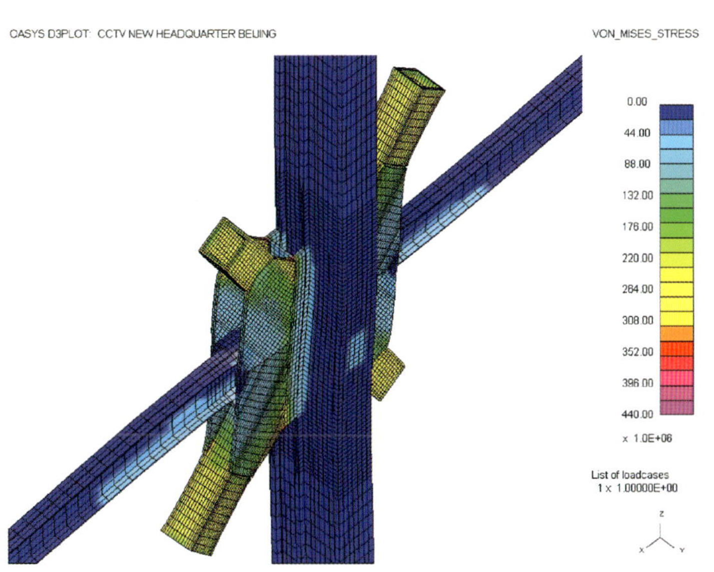

Perhaps the biggest challenge for the Arup team was the linking of the two towers, towards the end of the construction phase. With expansion and contraction of the structure caused by the extremes of hot and cold weather in Beijing, it was of paramount importance that the new headquarters of CCTV's design and engineering take into consideration the way the building would behave in its partially-constructed form, including expansion and contraction of the steel used at the top of the towers. Arup specified that the joining of both towers had to be done very early in the morning when both towers would be at a uniform temperature, before the sun started to rise, and with movements caused by the environment at a minimum.

Prior to the joining of the towers, Arup specified five days of monitoring the global and relative movements so the correct dimensions of the linking elements could be correctly predicted. Final adjustments were made to the length of the linking elements prior to installation, as it was vital that the towers were fixed together in a space of a few minutes. The final join was done at 8am on a cold winter's morning when the steel was at its most uniform temperature.

With the structures linked, it is much easier to appreciate the shared vision of OMA and Arup: to create a building that formed a loop in its internal workings, as well as in its external structure. This monumental structure signals the uniquely modern status of China Central Television and dominates Beijing's revitalised central business district.

(Opposite top) Lifting a steel element into place on the overhang–CCTV's unique structural form takes shape.

(Opposite bottom) A detail of the overhang as it begins to emerge from one of CCTV's towers.

(Right) Photograph showing the installation of the final connecting piece of the CCTV overhang in December 2007, the moment the continuous loop was joined.

(Following pages) A view of the overhang.

Nokia Green Building

(Opposite) View of the office space and communal atrium.

(Below) Cross section showing natural ventilation and daylight shading.

Known as the Nokia Green Building, Nokia China's new headquarters is the first newly-constructed commercial office building in China to be awarded a Leadership in Energy and Environmental Design (LEED) certificate by the United States Green Building Council.[1] With office space for 2,300 employees and a research and development centre for the company, the 70,000 square metre building is designed around sustainability and energy efficiency.

Arup's involvement in the project was broad, providing a range of services that included building sustainability consultancy, masterplanning, architectural design, structural engineering, mechanical, electrical, fire, lighting and acoustics. A crucial aspect of the design involved the use of advanced building physics to analyse the way materials would perform on the site, which helped to determine the most appropriate solutions and reduce wastage.

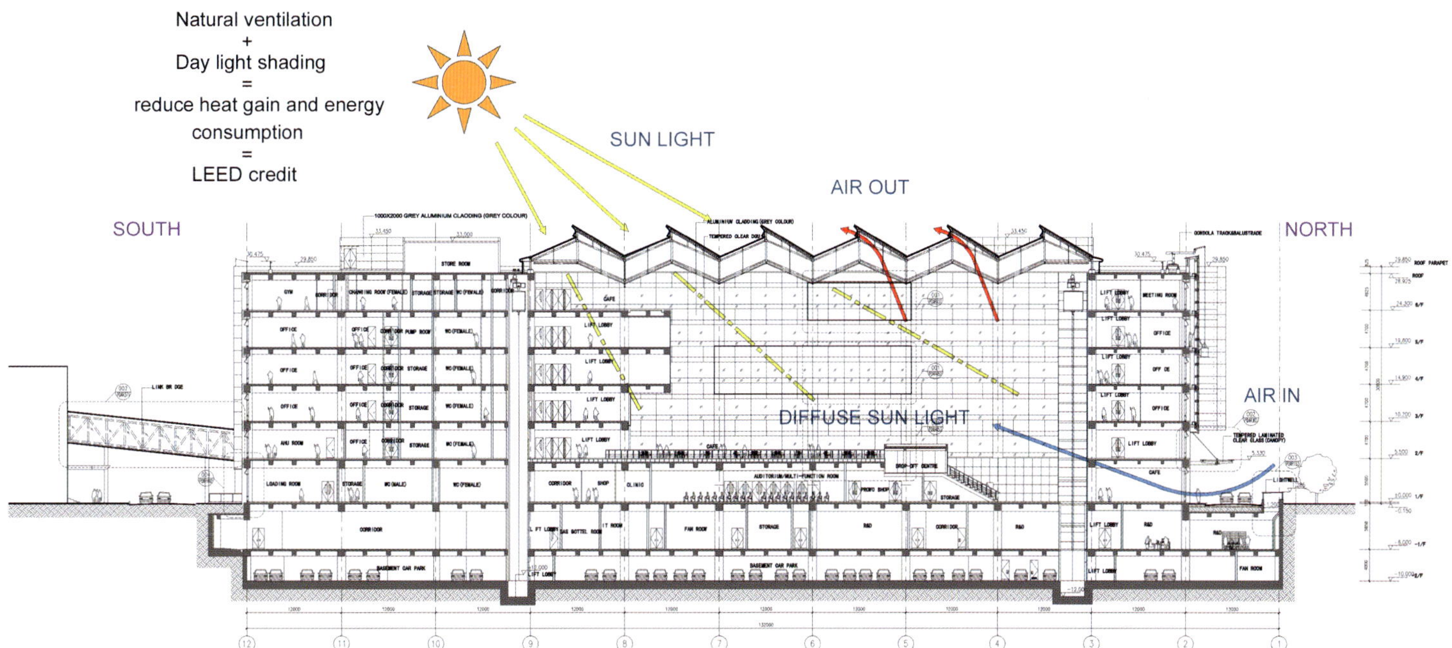

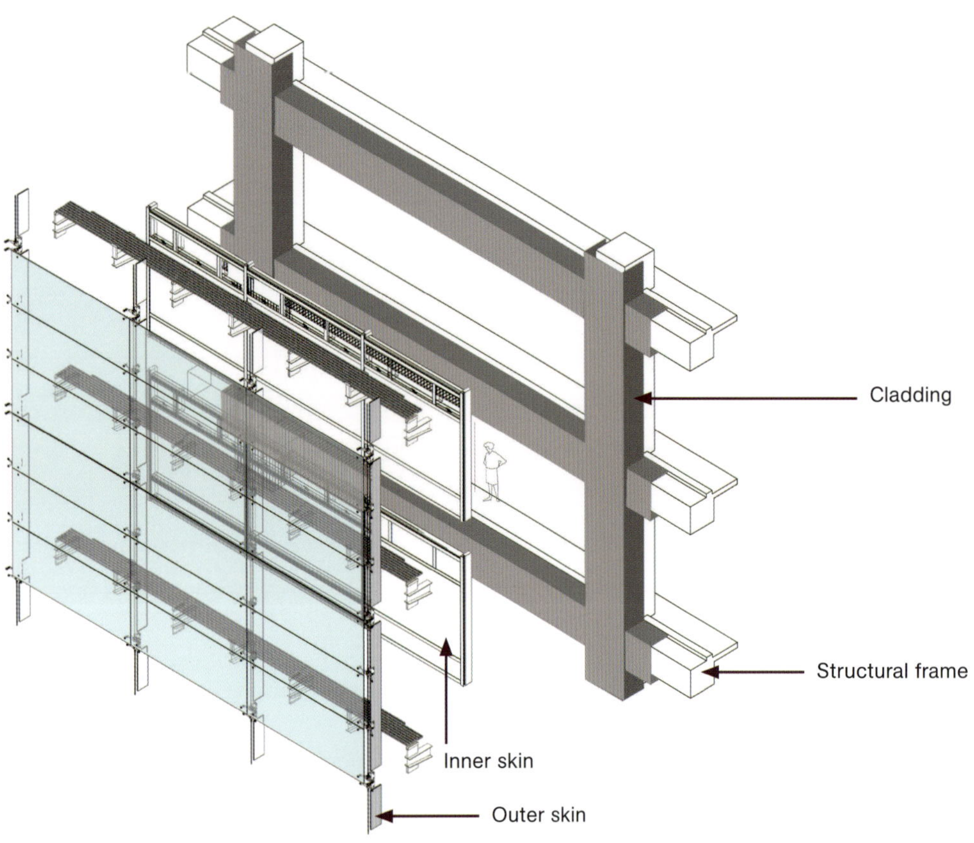

(Top) The double 'curtain wall' system consists of an internal double-glazed unit, a single-glazed external skin and a controllable ventilated cavity.

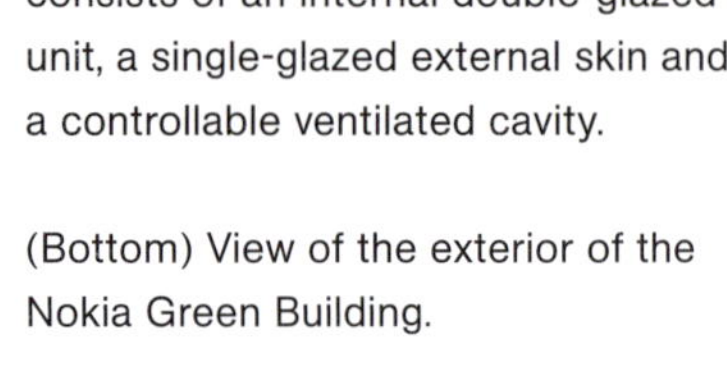

(Bottom) View of the exterior of the Nokia Green Building.

(Opposite left) The internal curtain wall provides thermal insulation, protection and ventilation. The internal skin consists of double-glazed tempered glass and a powder-coated anodised aluminium transom and mullion. The curtain wall is set on the building gridlines. Thermal insulation material is used for thermal protection enclosed by a powder-coated aluminium cladding panel.

(Opposite right) The external skins are mainly installed on the east, west and north elevations with partial coverage on the south elevation from level two onwards. The outer skin of the double-skin facade uses spider fixing. Fritted glass (ceramic painted glass) allows a degree of transparency while at the same time providing shading to reduce heat gain. The smooth facade prevents attachment of dust—a serious problem in Beijing.

The sustainability design strategy for the campus took into consideration the climatic conditions of the area, natural light and ventilation, and used recycled materials where possible. Numerous water conservation devices, double-layer glass walls and a significant number of advanced design techniques have resulted in a building that should reduce water use by 37 per cent and energy consumption by 20 per cent compared with typical commercial buildings.

The glass facades of the six-storey building have a temperature-controlled cavity between their panes. This works with the natural heat from the sun and the building's air conditioning system, to prevent the impact of outdoor temperatures being felt inside. While the east, west and north facades all require an inner and outer skin, the south wall only required a partial outer skin to achieve the same level of performance, thanks to its orientation.

1 The LEED Building Rating System provides a set of standards for environmentally sustainable construction and is aimed at encouraging and accelerating the global adoption of sustainable green building and development practices.

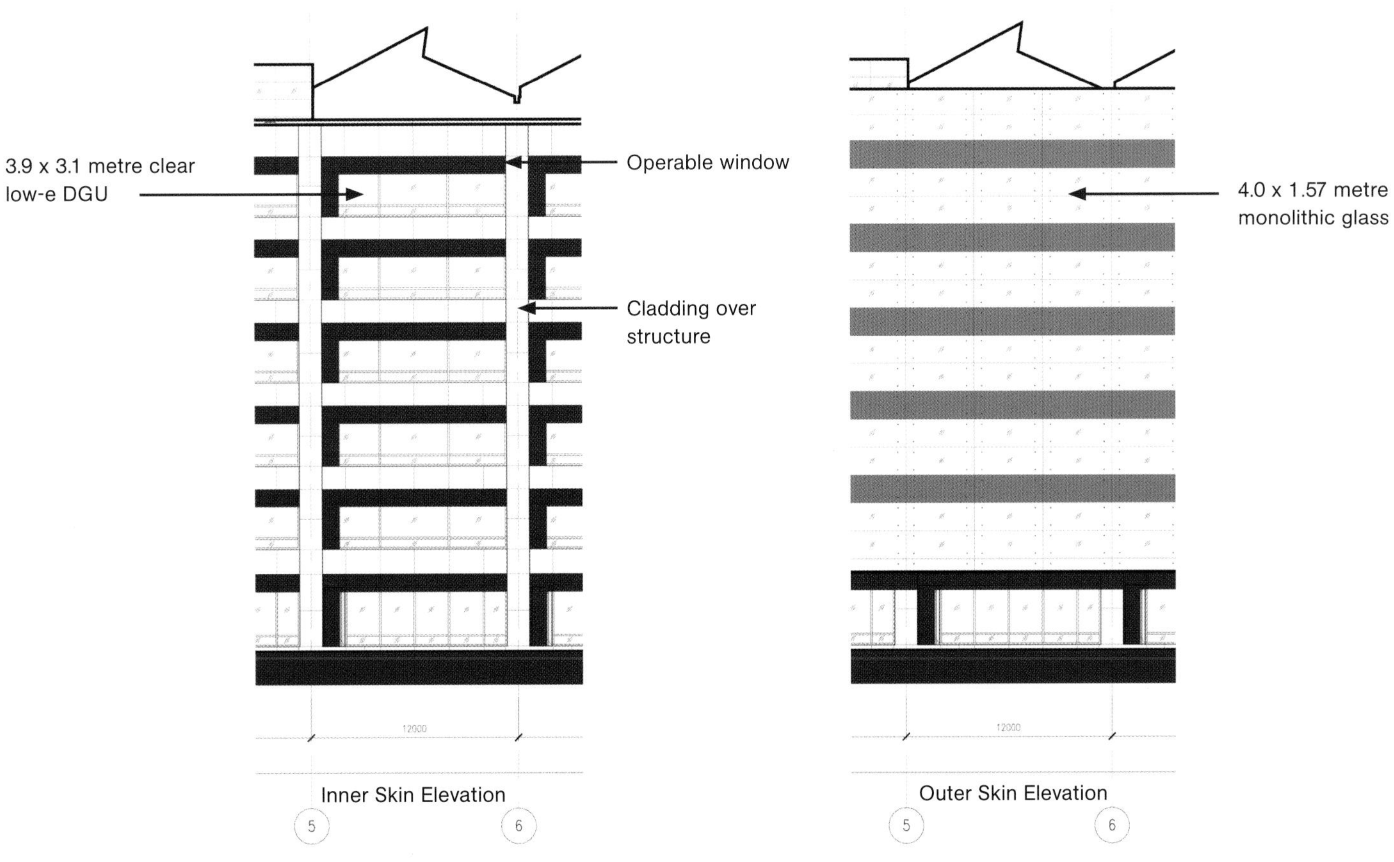

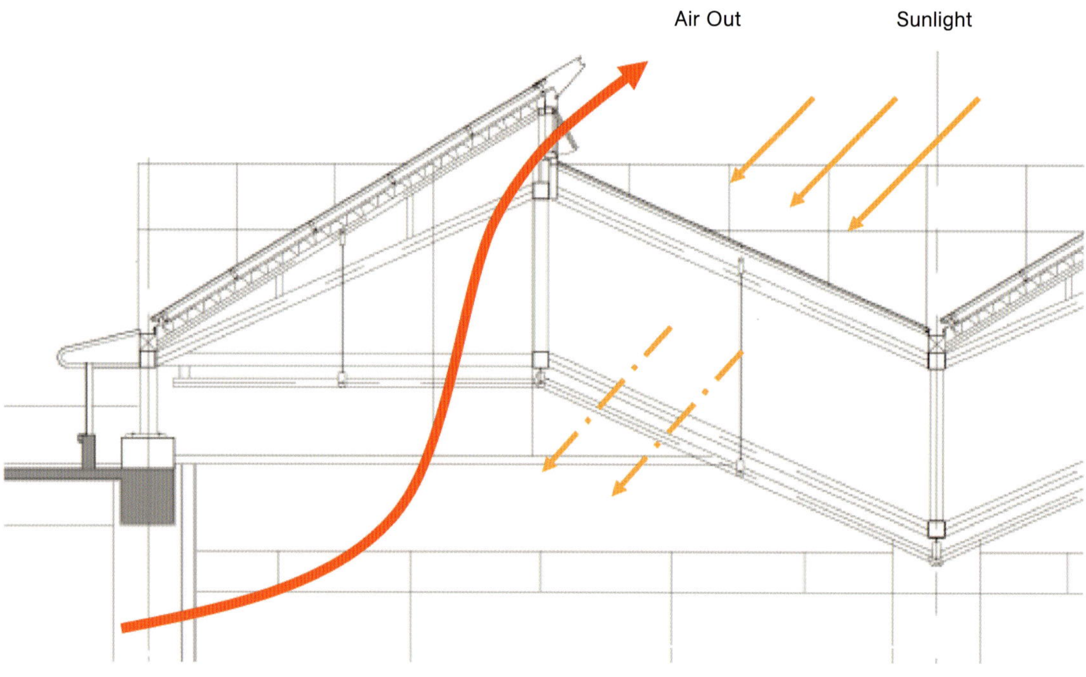

Heated air is vented through the atrium's openings.

Sunlight passes through the louvres, which provide shade, prevent glare and reduce heat gain.

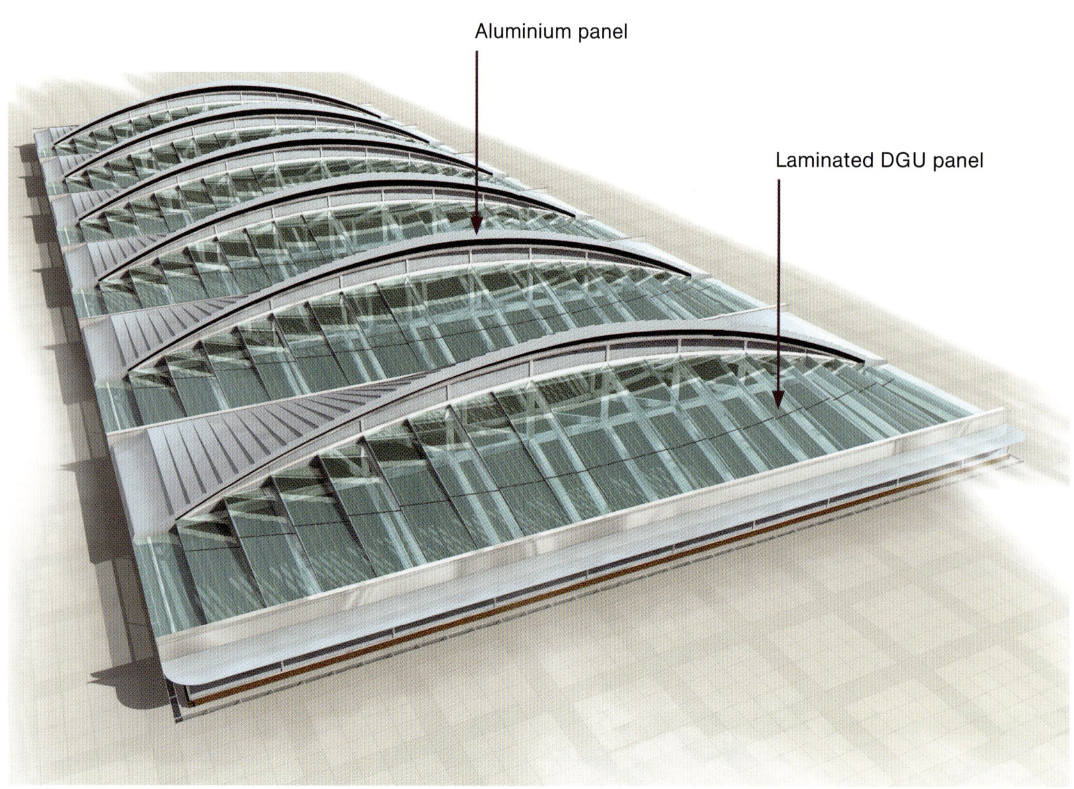

(Opposite top) Thanks to skylights—which are the main feature of the building envelope—energy efficiency is achieved even with a large portion of the facade being glazed to allow external views and daylight to penetrate. The skylights occupy 12 per cent of the total rooftop and are particularly efficient.

(Opposite bottom) External perspective. For the portion of the roof that is opaque, aluminium cladding with polyphony insulation board is used to reduce the heat transmitted.

(Above) Skylights and a large communal atrium provide natural light and ventilation throughout the building. The headquarters also has underground parking, a reserved parking area for environmentally-friendly cars, and a secure bicycle parking area.

KATO

China World Trade Center Phase 3

(Previous pages) The facade details of the China World Trade Center Phase 3.

(Opposite) Ongoing construction showing the complex steel and concrete structures.

(Below) Construction shot of the China World Trade Center Phase 3 at dusk showing how close it is to the China Central Television (CCTV) headquarters on the right.

At a height of 330 metres, the China World Trade Center (CWTC) Phase 3 is the tallest building in Beijing and is one of the focal points of Beijing's central business district. Across the street stands the new headquarters of China Central Television (CCTV), the structure that challenges traditional skyscraper design. Together, these two buildings are beacons of the city's newly revitalised business district.

Arup is the common link between the two. While the new headquarters of CCTV challenges preconceptions about a skyscraper's form, CWTC Phase 3 is no less challenging. It is one of the tallest buildings ever built in a seismic zone anywhere in the world. At 96 metres higher than CCTV's headquarters, CWTC Phase 3 stands head and shoulders above any of the other buildings in the business district. The engineering challenge was to ensure that it could be built safely.

Prior to CWTC Phase 3, the tallest buildings in Beijing were no higher than 200 metres. That buildings were not taller reflected the constraints on construction methods and engineering design due to the high prevalence of earthquakes in the region. While its role on CWTC Phase 3 didn't extend to the original design of the building form, Arup was instrumental in ensuring that the showpiece of the Beijing's International Finance Center would stand up.

First, Arup decided that CWTC Phase 3's structure would use more steel and less concrete, as the latter does not tolerate much movement, while steel is more ductile, with a much higher resistance to movement. But another variable Arup had to consider was that a building that used too much steel would actually be too soft; it would flex too much with movement and could be just as problematic as concrete. This led to the engineering conundrum of how to make the smartest use of the two materials so that the building is neither too stiff nor too soft.

While it is standard practice in most parts of the world to use concentric braced-steel frames in a building of this kind, Arup believed this was not ideal for CWTC Phase 3. While concentric bracing could resist very heavy lateral loads, it also draws in a lot of force into the beam column joints, which would be a significant problem in Beijing's seismic conditions. The Arup solution was to include, for each wall, one bay with a concentric brace that doesn't join to its opposite corner. This reduces the potential damage that the building would suffer during a strong earthquake.

(Left) Shear Plate Steel Wall. Building tall structures in high seismic areas should use less concrete, which cannot tolerate much movement. However, a pure steel building would be too soft and flex too much, so a balance has to be found. Arup suggested using a shear wall made of composite steel plate—the first of its kind in China—stretching from the basement levels up to the 16th floor. This, along with composite columns and steel beams and braces throughout the entire structure, formed the core of the building. A perimeter of more composite columns and beams added further robustness, but it was the application of the bracing that called for the most ingenuity.

(Opposite top) Workers on site, at one of the three levels at which the tower tapers are to give Phase 3 its distinctive profile.

(Opposite bottom) Workers appear as specks against the steel and glass facade.

国际贸易中心三期工程主楼模拟地震振动台试验

In a first for China, Arup suggested using a shear wall made of composite steel plate, stretching from basement levels up to the 16th floor. This, along with composite columns and steel beams and braces throughout all 74 floors of the entire building, forms the core of this shining, proud structure.

Other investigations had to be undertaken to test CWTC Phase 3's strength and flexibility. New techniques were used to examine the behaviour of the building under different seismic levels. Such comprehensive tests had not been undertaken in China before, provoking a great deal of interest in Beijing's planning community.

A 1:30 scale physical model was created where, under strict laboratory conditions, seismic waves were simulated through a 'shaking table test' to justify the analysis conducted by Arup. This test made use of a total of 46 sets of actual Beijing earthquake records, which were then used as measures by which to test the CWTC Phase 3 model. The results proved that the movement of the building under severe earthquake conditions was completely in accordance with Beijing's strict structural safety requirements.

Over and above the contribution that CWTC Phase 3's engineering design makes to the Beijing skyline, the building is also a good example of a development that creates stronger links with the community around it, with state-of-the-art offices, retail space, entertainment venues and a six star hotel at the building's pinnacle. This is all contained in a tapered form that has an imposing mix of glass and steel. With its facade of faceted vertical glass and metal fins, the China World Trade Center Phase 3 significantly enhances Beijing's growing stock of international-standard office developments.

Shaking table test. To satisfy the experts' performance criteria, a 1:30 scale physical model was used in laboratory conditions. Seismic waves were simulated using a 'shaking table test' to justify the non-linear time history analysis carried out by Arup. The test showed that this analysis was sufficient to simulate the performance of the structure under various levels of earthquakes.

The sheer size of the building is revealed. At 330 metres in height, the China World Trade Center Phase 3 is the tallest building in north China.

Beijing South Rail Station

(Previous pages) Nightview of the Beijing South Rail Station while under construction.

(Opposite top) Artist's impression of the illuminated Station from the northwest looking along the central hall. Inspired by Beijing's famous temple of heaven the roof of the Station is symmetrical. A dramatic skylight runs along the central axis of the dome-shaped roof which is flanked by two separate side canopies.

(Below) An artist's impression revealing the structure of the side canopies and central hall roofs.

The new Beijing South Rail Station is a major architectural icon for China's capital city and is one of the largest stations in China, eventually catering for over 100 million passengers a year. It connects the capital with Shanghai and Tianjin, making Beijing accessible by rail to a catchment area of up to 270 million people. In a city being transformed in advance of the 2008 Beijing Olympic Games, the new terminal stands out as a symbol of Beijing's cultural and political pre-eminence.

Its striking design pays tribute to traditional Chinese architecture. The scalloped silhouette of the roof—which claims to being the largest transparent roof in the world—is strongly inspired by the Hall for Prayer for Good Harvests in Beijing's Temple of Heaven. With such a striking link to China's cultural heritage, the Beijing South Rail Station provides a welcome focus to an area of Beijing that is undergoing profound redevelopment.

(Previous pages) Exterior view of the northwest elevation at sunset.

(Opposite top) Artist's impression from the west.

(Opposite bottom) Detail of the canopy roof at the outer most span.

(Below) Artist's impression of a typical high-speed rail platform. The Beijing–Tianjin and Beijing–Shanghai high-speed railway lines begin here.

Six kilometres from the Forbidden City and three kilometres west of the Temple of Heaven, the new Station will handle over 30,000 travellers an hour at peak time, linking with national high-speed rail lines and local and regional services. The Beijing–Tianjin and Beijing–Shanghai high-speed railway lines begin here, and the Station also links with the Beijing Metro Lines M4 and M14. It also connects with vehicular transport including, taxis, buses and private cars. It has 40 taxi bays, 30 bus pickup areas, and an 800-space car park.

The Station's elliptical design was conceived by architects Terry Farrell and Partners, winning an international competition in 2003. With the large volume of people and huge scale of the building—500 metres by 380 metres in size—their approach was one of a clear, simple and people-oriented design. In practice, this meant creating a building with efficient passenger flow, convenient interchanges and connections. The Station is open plan to create generous views and ensure that other transport links to the city—buses, taxis, light rail and underground systems—are readily accessible. An environmental approach ensures that the Station uses as much natural light as possible, helping to provide a simple solution to energy conservation. Level one of the Station is a concourse for rail passengers, while on the ground floor are the tracks and platform. Below that, in the basement, is the transfer hub.

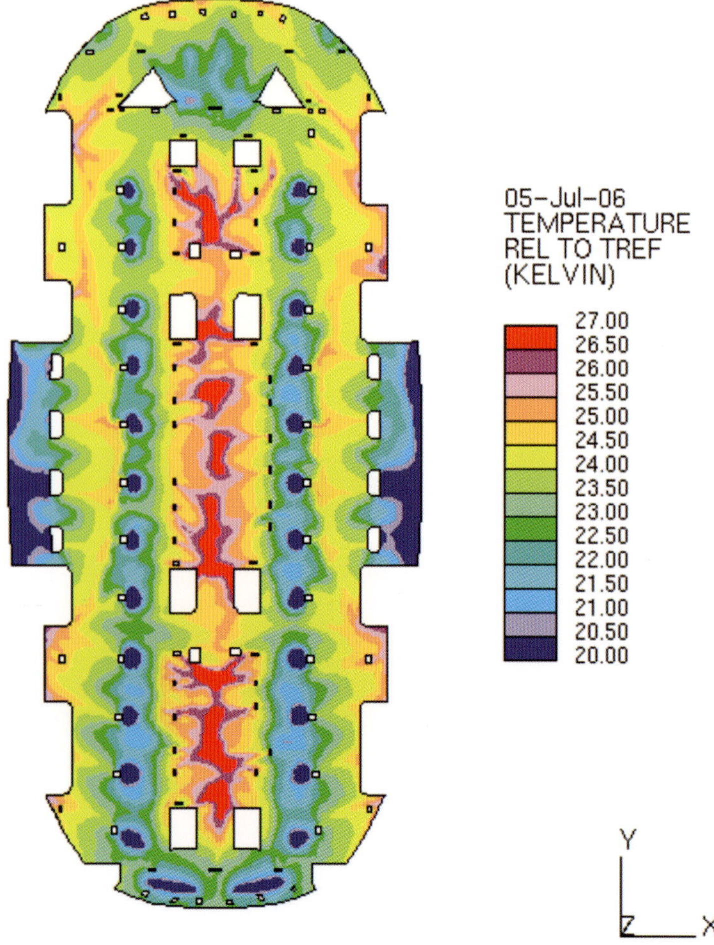

(Top) The CFD model of the elevated waiting hall and arrangement of air conditioning totem associated with air supply nozzles.

(Bottom) Indoor temperature distribution of the elevated waiting hall by using spot cooling.

Beijing South Rail Station has a total construction area of 22 million square metres, which comprises a 50,400 square metre waiting hall 40 metres in height. The elevated waiting hall can accommodate 10,500 people at any one time. The building envelope of the roof structure comprises composite aluminum material plates coupled with insulation material. This high-intensity, tough and good decorative material is used to achieve both green and aesthetic ends. The design considerations for the building envelope of the Station, such as solar heat gain, shading devices and the thermal comfort of passengers is established by Integrated Environmental Simulation (IES) and Computational Fluid Dynamics (CFD), as shown.

Arup was brought in to provide a broad range of multi-disciplinary services to the project: specialist input on the trackway and platform designs, building physics and MEP (mechanical, electric and public health) design of the Station, and wind engineering and acoustic design. This included developing the initial structural scheme for the roof with its Chinese design partners, and managing the wind tunnel testing for the building's unique form. Arup's experts used advanced engineering techniques employing computational fluid dynamic modelling to assess air quality at the raised access roads around the Station, together with detailed investigation into the Station's combined cooling, heating and power system, its airflow and annual energy consumption.

From the beginning, the project presented unique fire risk challenges, and Arup's specialist fire engineers were engaged to take a performance-based approach to the problem. This was necessary because the Beijing South Rail Station's large spaces, multi-use occupancies and architectural space planning are not addressed by the current Chinese fire code. But, by analysing and testing the physical performance of the building in a broad range of fire situations, Arup could ensure the Station has a high level of fire safety.

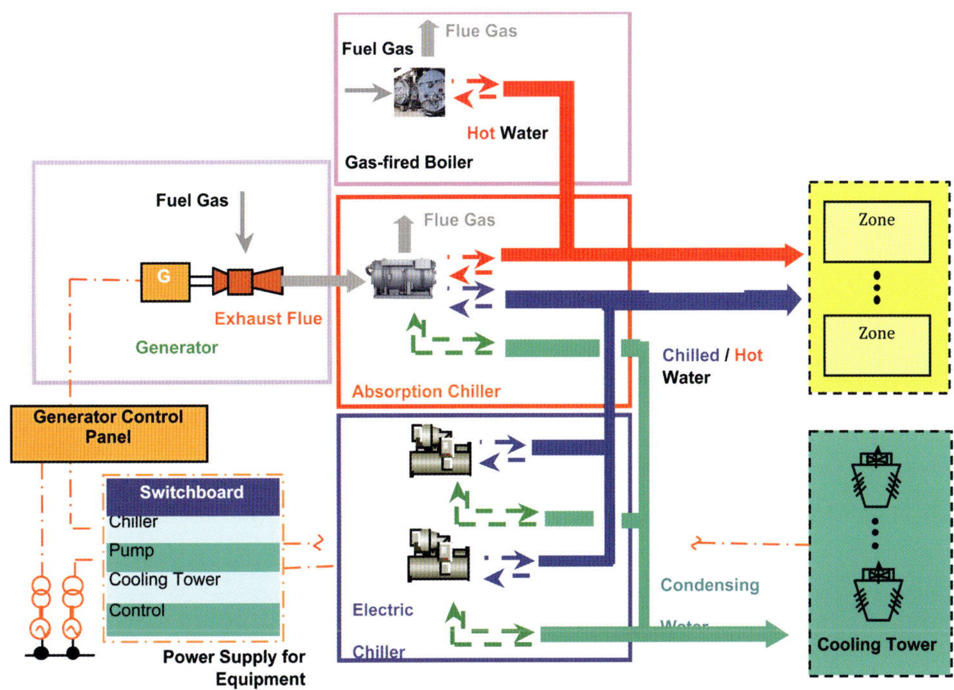

The schematic design of the Combined Heat and Power (CHP) system. CHP, also known as co-generation, is the name applied to processes which from a single stream of fuel simultaneously generate heat and electrical power. CHP uses either a gas turbine or gas fired engine to drive an electricity generator and makes practical use of the heat which is an inevitable by-product. This heat can be used for making process steam and for cooling using absorption chillers.

The overall efficiency of CHP systems can be in excess of 80 per cent, which is far better than conventional power stations. This leads to considerable reductions in emissions of carbon dioxide, nitrogen oxides and sulphur dioxide. Therefore, CHP systems not only increase the security of supply, but also improve the environmental impact of energy generation. Beijing South Rail Station utilises a CHP arrangement to provide electricity, cooling (in summer) or heating (in winter) to the Station and ancillary building.

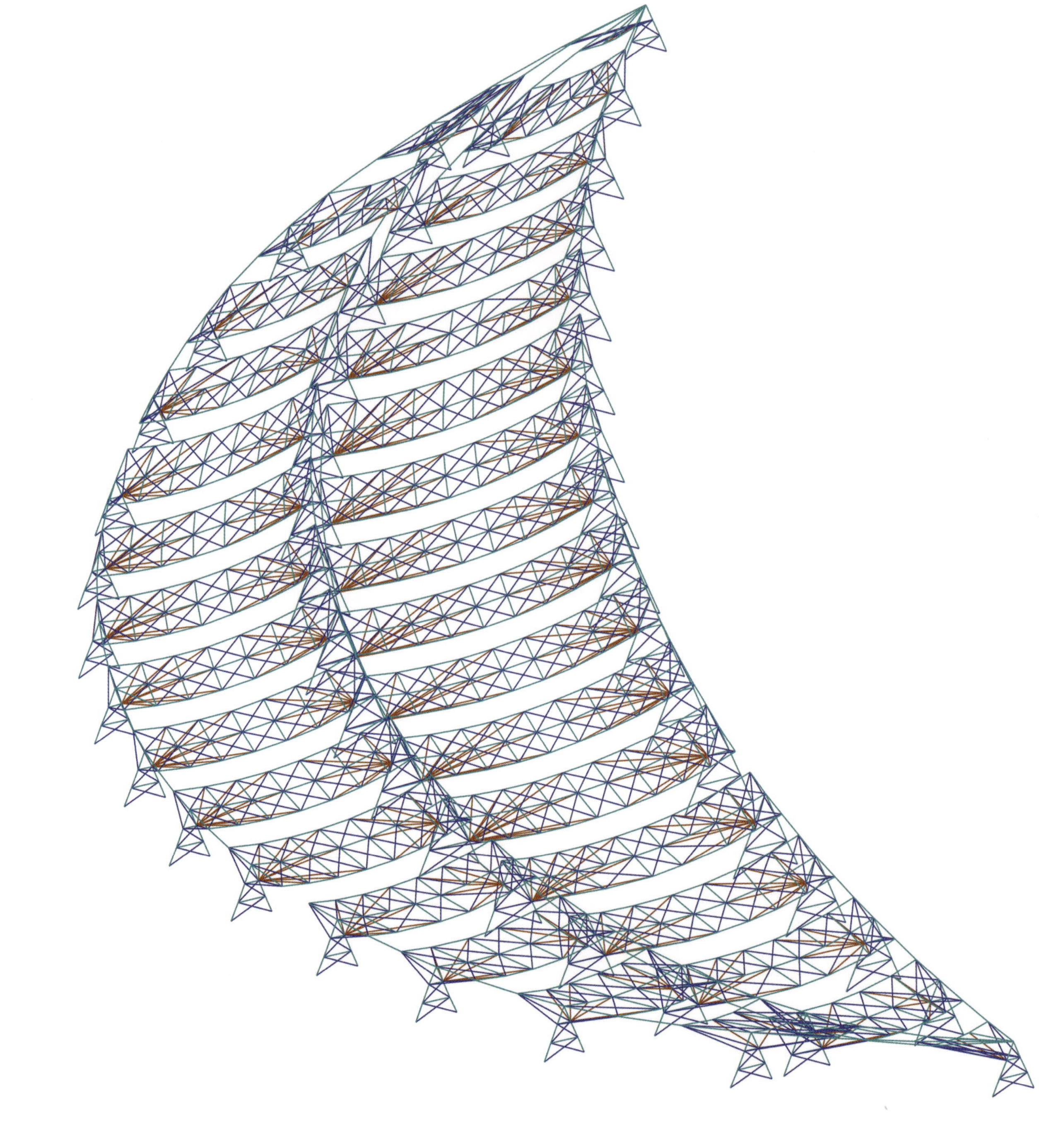

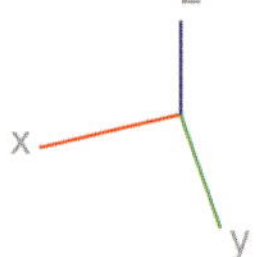
z
x
y

However, it is Arup's work on the vast curvaceous roof that will impress most visitors to the Beijing South Rail Station. Arup took responsibility for approval of the schematic, preliminary, and detailed design of the multi-span, cable-stayed roof. At up to 40 metres tall and spanning between 350 and 500 metres, its scale is vast. The cables used in the roof alone cross spans of between 66 and 70 metres. A counterbalance to this vastness is the roof's transparency. 240 tonnes of polycarbonate sheeting give the Station its light, airy feel, providing an elegant, column-free shelter for the platforms.

With a clean, modern look, the Beijing South Rail Station is a symbol of Beijing's modernising ambition, while at the same time paying homage to China's traditional architectural past.

(Opposite) A 3-D analytical model of the main side canopy roofs.

(Top) Artist's impression of the end glazed wall area of the Central Hall at the southeast side of the Station.

(Bottom) Artist's impression of the platform area under the canopy roof.

GreenPix Zero Energy Media Wall

(Opposite) Detailed view of the individual photovoltaic arrays.

(Below left) The photovoltaic cells feed energy into the building systems during the day–reducing energy costs for the building–while also acting as an effective shading device to protect the building from excessive heat gain.

(Below right) At night, the new envelope will release the energy accumulated throughout the day in the form of bursts of light, transforming the facade into a glowing beacon and making the building an overwhelming visual experience within the nightscape of Beijing.

In west Beijing, the city's thriving artist community has a new and unusual 'canvas' on which to experiment: the GreenPix Zero Energy Media Wall. It is the largest colour light-emitting diode (LED) light wall in the world. This virtuoso feat of engineering and lighting design is also a striking example of energy efficiency, with the photovoltaic arrays on the building capturing twice as much energy from the sun than the lighting facade consumes.

The Chinese contemporary art scene has experienced a major expansion in recent years, with many artists now competing in the international contemporary art market. With significant Chinese art exhibitions taking place in Europe during 2008, the world is beginning to take note. Beijing has quickly become a significant destination for art buyers—in particular, the city's 798 Art District.

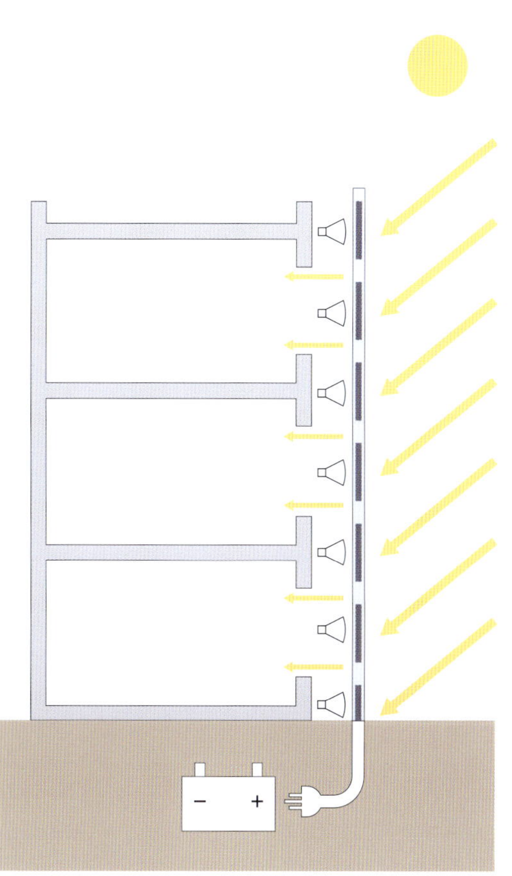

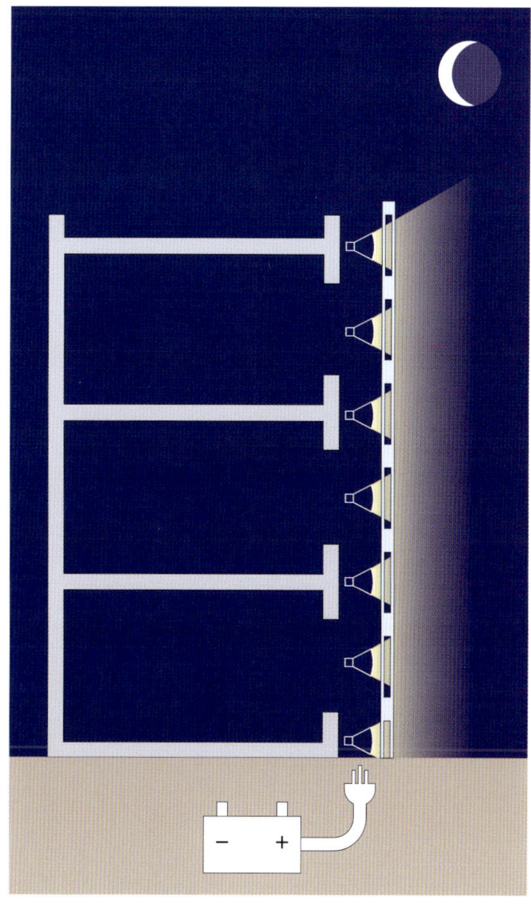

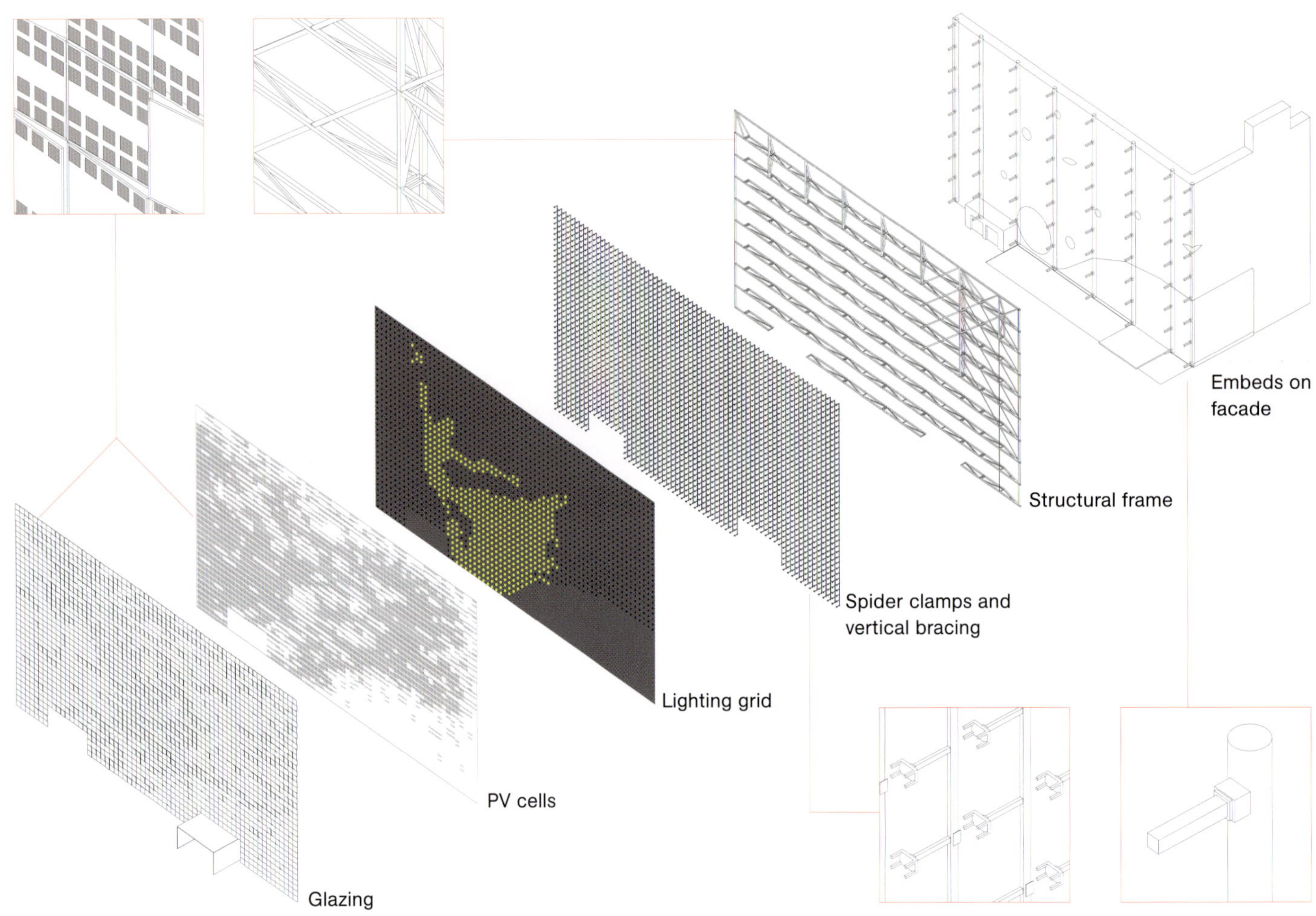

(Above) The lightweight facade structure supported from the existing building is strong enough to cope with seismic loads. Layers of photovoltaics generating energy, subtle glass characteristics and an innovative LED lighting system are compacted together into a technological skin that radically changes appearance between day and night.

(Opposite) The subtle interplay of light and glass creates a sense of depth on the facade of the GreenPix Zero Energy Media Wall.

The GreenPix Zero Energy Media Wall creates a major new focus for the community of digital artists. The 60 metre by 33 metre laminated glass facade contains photovoltaic arrays, which harvest solar energy by day. It incorporates a futuristic lighting system, capable of displaying moving images on a 'screen' made up from 2,000 individually programmable LED colour nodes. Offering media and digital artists an almost infinite range of possibilities, the media wall particularly lends itself to creative interpretation.

Like any new structure in Beijing, the GreenPix Zero Energy Media Wall has been engineered to comply with Beijing's seismic regulations, and is entirely self-supporting. The darker panels accommodate denser PV arrays; the lightest panels contain none, while slight variations in the angle between each panel lend an interesting textural quality to the structure by day, said to be reminiscent of the dappling of sun on water.

(Opposite) The 2,000 individually programmable LED nodes offer artists an almost infinite range of lighting possiblities.

(Below) Detail of the 60 x 33 metre laminated glass facade of the GreenPix Zero Energy Media wall.

The design called for a subtle interplay of light and glass, to create a sense of depth beyond the physical surface of the glass. Using sophisticated computer modelling and analysis, Arup was able to develop a combination of glass and lighting involving coloured LED nodes spaced behind the glass exterior. When illuminated at night, the facade would 'de-materialise' and appear to glow like water lit from within. Mock-ups were then used to refine the more subtle and more elusive characteristics of the glass.

GreenPix launches in the summer of 2008 with a series of video art installations. The hope is that it will galvanise an energetic artistic community and produce a valued, ever-changing public work of art that becomes part of the everyday lives of residents.

Arup worked with New York architects Simone Giostra & Partners to produce a design that not only showcases the newest technologies in lighting and solar energy capture, but also pioneers their use together.

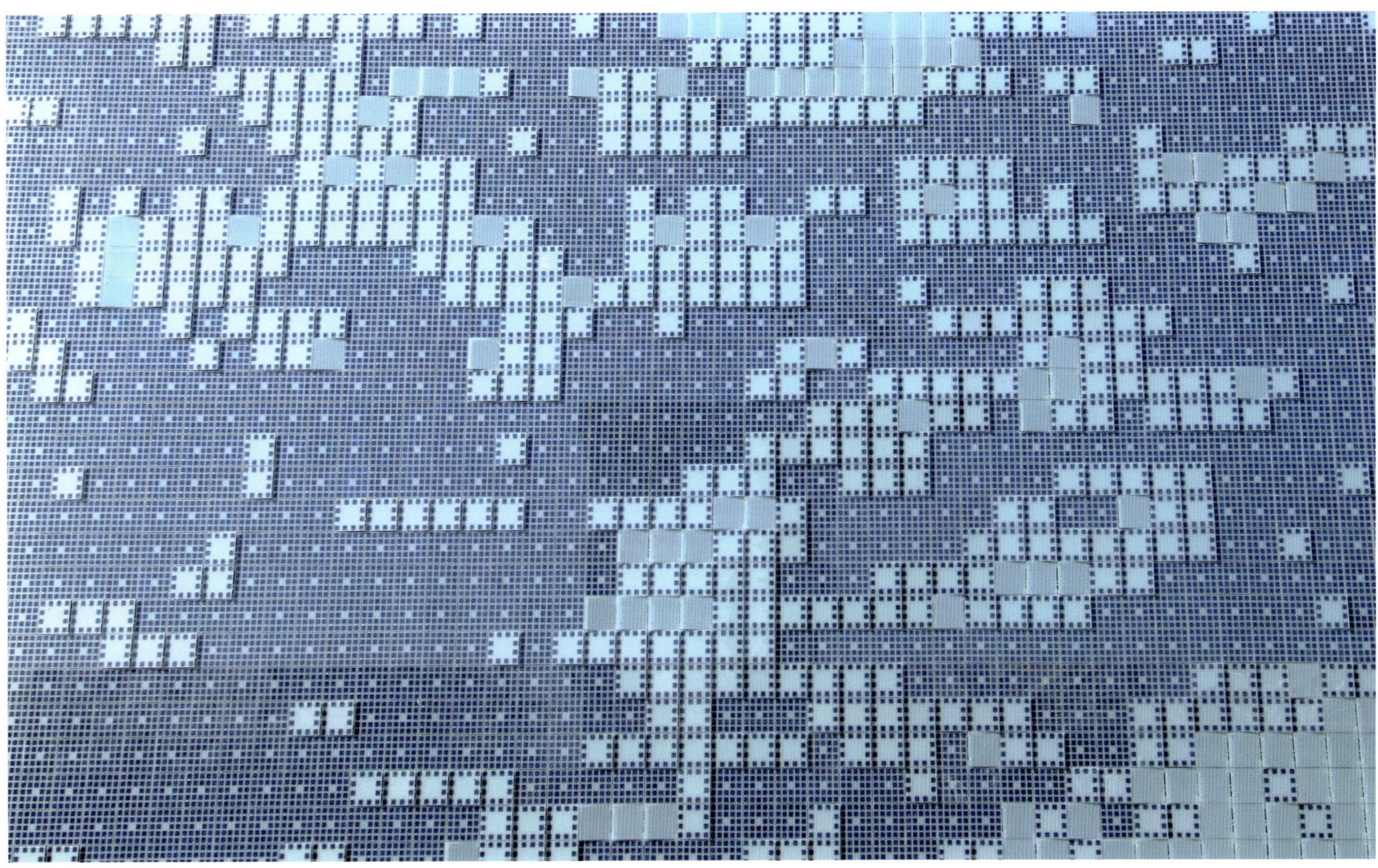

本书的出版得到了很多人的帮助，我们要感谢以下人士：

- 委托我们从事这些项目的十大客户
- 数十名工程师和来自本地设计单位的建筑师，他们才华横溢，与奥雅纳一道完成了项目的设计
- 数百名建模师，他们帮助我们梦想成真
- 数千名全身心投入的奥雅纳设计师、顾问和工程师，他们让建筑成为了现实
- 数万名建筑工人，他们不知疲倦地工作，按时完成了施工
- 全球数十亿观看奥运会的观众，以及
- 一千六百万北京市民，他们摒息关注着新建筑在古城中崛起。

This book would not have been possible without the involvement and input of many people. We would like to acknowledge the

- ten visionary clients who commissioned the projects
- dozens of brilliant architects and engineers of the local design institutes who worked with Arup to design them
- hundreds of model-makers that helped test the flights of fancy
- thousands of dedicated Arup designers, consultants and engineers who made the structures a reality
- tens of thousands of construction workers who worked tirelessly to finish it all on time
- billions of people watching the Games around the world and, not least, the
- 16 million people of Beijing for watching, with bated-breath, as the new has emerged from the old.

p. 9 ©Arup
p. 11 ©Skidmore Owings & Merrill
p. 12 ©Arup/Ben McMillan
p. 14 ©Arup/Ben McMillan
p. 15 ©Arup/Ben McMillan
p. 16 ©OMA/Ole Scheeren and Rem Koolhaas
p. 23 left ©Arup/Frank P Palmer
p. 23 right ©Arup/Ben McMillan
p. 24 ©Arup/Ben McMillan
p. 25 ©Arup/Ben McMillan
p. 26 top ©Arup/Frank P Palmer
p. 26 bottom left ©Arup
p. 26 bottom right
©Arup/Martin Saunders Photography
p. 27 ©Marcel Lam
p. 28 ©Bernardo De Niz
p. 29 top ©Arup/Martin Saunders Photography
p. 29 bottom ©Arup/Chas Pope
p. 30 ©Arup/Martin Saunders Photography
p. 31 ©Arup/Martin Saunders Photography
p. 32 ©Arup/Frank P Palmer
p. 41 ©TFP Farrells/KWP
p. 42 ©Zhou Ruogu Architecture Photography
p. 47 ©Arup
p. 51 ©Arup
p. 53 ©Arup
p. 54 ©Arup/Frank P Palmer
p. 57 ©Arup/Frank P Palmer
p. 58 ©Arup/Frank P Palmer
p. 65 ©Simone Giostra & Partners Inc/
Arup/Zhou Ruogu Architecture Photography
pp. 66 and 67 ©Arup/Ben McMillan
p. 68 ©Herzog & De Meuron
p. 69 ©Jeremy Stern
pp. 70 and 71 ©Arup/Ben McMillan
p. 72 top ©Arup/Martin Saunders Photography
p. 72 bottom ©Arup/Ben McMillan
p. 74 top ©Marcel Lam
p. 74 bottom ©Jeremy Stern
p. 76 and 77 ©Arup/Ben McMillan
pp. 78 and 79 ©Zhou Ruogu Architecture Photography
p. 80 ©Bernardo De Niz
p. 81 ©Arup
p. 82 ©Arup/PTW/CCDI
p. 83 ©Arup/Ben McMillan
p. 84 ©Arup/Ben McMillan
p. 85 ©Arup/PTW/CCDI
p. 86 ©Arup/PTW/CCDI
p. 87 ©Arup
pp. 88 and 89 ©Arup/Ben McMillan
p. 90 ©Arup/Ben McMillan
pp. 92 and 93 ©Marcel Lam
pp. 94 and 95 ©Arup/Ben McMillan
p. 96 ©Arup/PTW/CCDI
p. 97 ©Arup/PTW/CCDI
p. 98 ©Arup/Frank P Palmer
p. 99 ©Arup
p. 100 ©Arup/Zhou Ruogu Architecture Photography
p. 101 ©Integrated Design
Associates Architects & Designers
pp. 102 and 103 ©Arup/Martin Saunders Photography
p. 104 ©RMJM Ltd
p. 105 left ©RMJM Ltd
p. 105 right ©RMJM Ltd
p. 107 ©Arup/Martin Saunders Photography
p. 108 ©Arup/James Harris Photography
pp. 110 and 111 ©NFA JV
p. 112 ©Arup
p. 113 ©Arup/Martin Saunders Photography
p. 114 ©Arup/Frank P Palmer
p. 115 ©Arup
p. 116 top ©NFA JV
p. 116 bottom ©Arup
p. 117 top ©Arup
p. 117 middle ©Arup
p. 117 bottom ©Arup
p. 118 left ©Arup
p. 118 right ©Arup
p. 119 ©Arup/Frank P Palmer
pp. 120 and 121 ©Arup/Ben McMillan
p. 122 ©Arup/Ben McMillan
p. 123 ©NFA JV
pp. 124 and 125 ©Arup/
OMA/Ole Scheeren and Rem Koolhaas
p. 126 ©Arup/Frank P Palmer
p. 127 ©Arup/OMA/Ole Scheeren and Rem Koolhaas
p. 128 ©Arup/OMA/Ole Scheeren and Rem Koolhaas
p. 129 ©Arup/Chas Pope
p. 130 top ©Arup
p. 131 left ©Arup
p. 131 right ©Arup/James Harris Photography
p. 132 top ©Arup
p. 132 bottom ©Arup/Frank P Palmer
p. 133 ©Arup/Chas Pope
pp. 134 and 135 ©Arup/Frank P Palmer
p. 136 ©Arup/Jerry Lee
p. 137 ©Arup
p. 138 top ©Arup

p. 138 bottom ©Arup
p. 139 left ©Arup
p. 139 right ©Arup
p. 140 top ©Arup
p. 140 bottom ©Arup
p. 141 ©Arup/Jerry Lee
pp. 142 and 143 Martin Saunders Photography
p. 144 ©Arup/Frank P Palmer
p. 145 ©Arup/Frank P Palmer
p. 146 ©Arup
p. 147 top ©Arup/Frank P Palmer
p. 147 bottom ©Arup
p. 148 ©Arup
p. 150 ©Arup/Frank P Palmer
p. 152 and 153 ©Arup/James Harris Photography
p. 154 top ©TFP Farrells/KWP
pp. 154 and 155 bottom ©TFP Farrells/KWP
pp. 156 and 157 ©Arup/
Zhou Ruogu Architecture Photography
p. 158 top ©TFP Farrells/KWP
p. 158 bottom ©Arup/
Zhou Ruogu Architecture Photography
p. 159 ©TFP Farrells/KWP
p. 160 top and bottom ©Arup
p. 161 ©Arup
p. 162 ©Arup
p. 163 top and bottom ©TFP Farrells/KWP
p. 164 ©Arup/Simone Giostra/Frank P Palmer
p. 165 left and right ©Simone Giostra & Partners Inc
p. 166 ©Simone Giostra & Partners Inc
p. 167 ©Simone Giostra/Arup/
Zhou Ruogu Architecture Photography
p. 168 ©Simone Giostra/Arup/
Zhou Ruogu Architecture Photography
p. 169 ©Simone Giostra/Arup/Frank P Palmer

Black Dog Publishing Limited
10A Acton Street
London WC1X 9NG
United Kingdom

Tel: +44 (0) 20 7713 5097
Fax: +44 (0) 20 7713 8682
info@blackdogonline.com
www.blackdogonline.com

ISBN: 978 1 906155 47 6

British Library Cataloguing-in-Publication Data.
A CIP record for this book is available from
the British Library.

Designed by Matthew Pull with Ana Estrougo
at Black Dog Publishing

Printed in Italy

Black Dog Publishing Limited, London, UK, is an environmentally responsible company. *Solutions For A Modern City: Arup In Beijing* is printed on Fedrigoni Symbol Freelife, Fedrigoni Freelife Cento, Burgo R400 and Burgo Selena, all of which are FSC certified papers.

architecture art design
fashion history photography
theory and things

www.blackdogonline.com